W0296542

STARK

ABITUR-TRAINING ENGLISCH

Nach der neuen Prüfungsordnung

Liam Cleary

Textaufgaben

Literarische Texte und Sachtexte

STARK

ISBN: 3-89449-651-7

© 2004 by Stark Verlagsgesellschaft mbH
D-85318 Freising · Postfach 1852 · Tel. (0 81 61) 1790
Nachdruck verboten!

Contents

Author: Liam Cleary

Access to English!

Before you start working on the texts and worksheets provided in this book it is important to consider your general approach to studying English as a subject for the "Abitur" and for the "Klausuren" you will have to tackle. Remember that to be good at a language, be it in written or oral exercises, you must have contact with the language. If you are serious about doing well in English, you must start putting the following tips into practice, all of which are designed to bring you into more frequent contact with the language and improve your final grade.

Tip 1: Your attitude to English: Be positive!

Remind yourself how much **you already know** and how **determined you are to learn more**. If you make a mistake while speaking or writing English either forget about it and keep going or make a mental note to find out the correct way of using the term in question. It is the amount of **correct English** you can write and speak that counts.

Tip 2: Remember: You are learning for life

Keep in mind that when improving your English you are also going to benefit long-term, not just for the exam ahead. English will always keep coming back into your life, be it at a job interview or a holiday barbecue in America, Ireland, Britain, Australia, Canada or wherever else English is spoken. Much of the knowledge we learn at school is of limited use in later life. That is not the case with English.

Tip 3: Peak at the right time

Students often forget that you can both learn and, for want of a better word, unlearn a language. At any given moment in time your English is only as good as your contact to, and use of, the language. If you do not use a language you start to forget it. When preparing for your exam you must slowly but surely increase your daily use of English so that you peak just before the day you sit down to take the English paper or do the oral English test.

Tip 4: Improve your study approach

Listen, Read, Speak, Write.

- Watch **English-language TV** channels e.g. CNN, Bloomberg, Sky NEWS, BBC World, CNBC, and BBC Parliament. They are not always the most exciting but most of them deal with up-to-date topics. In this respect satellite offers a greater range than cable television.
- Find the **BBC World service** and other **radio stations** and begin listening to them, starting with a quarter of an hour session, e.g. News about Britain, and then increasing the length of time you spend at the task. It will be difficult at first but **you must stick at it**. The World Service is a good choice because the English used by the newsreaders is easy to understand. Make notes of useful words or phrases as you listen.
- Buy **audio cassettes** in English. The best ones to buy are not actually language courses as you may be past that stage by now. Consider buying books on tape for native-speaking teenagers a bit younger than yourself. The language in Harry Potter for instance is superb if you want to improve and the reader, Stephen Fry, is excellent.
- Another source of English is an **audio file from a website**. Listening to such sources of English allows you to go to the websites you are actually interested in.
- If you are lucky enough to live in a big town or city there will frequently be **English-language film evenings** or **readings by authors or politicians** in your area. The British Council is a good source of information for this. Get up and go to these events. It pays off.
- Buy **English-language books**. The choice is huge, be it from shops or on line. Choose something that interests you and will not be too hard. You don't have to buy James Joyce, Martin Amis or Jane Smiley first off. Try the bestsellers list. You may learn more from Nick Hornby, Maeve Binchy or J. K. Rowling. The book should interest you but it's important the level of English is not too difficult or you will be put off by it.
- **Read an English-language newspaper** or just some of the texts that appeal to you. The language in a tabloid paper such as The Daily Mail is probably easier – despite the use of slang and difficult headlines – than in the quality papers. The Guardian, Observer, Irish Times and The Independent belong to this latter group. Of the on-line newspapers I recommend The Economist and The Guardian (London). Study the articles for content and tone. Make summaries, note good phrases.

- In the months after Christmas go to **www.Amazon.co.uk** or some other website that sells books, look at their bestseller lists **and read the summaries and reviews** of such books as are on the list. Many Abitur texts come from current bestselling lists. It is worth your while keeping in touch and up to date with these.
- Speak English in class and out of class. If you are a quiet student who prefers to let others do the talking this is something you must get over and change. Don't be put off by mistakes, learn from them. You must keep trying if you are to succeed. Rome wasn't built in a day!
- See if you can meet some **native speakers** on a regular basis.
- Send **letters and e-mails** to people abroad. Every piece of contact helps.
- Consider spending a week of the **holidays** in your final year in an English-speaking area. If you manage to get there be sure and talk to people. Otherwise you may as well stay at home!

Tip 5: Do the worksheets in this book!

All the tips so far have concerned your general study of English. They will improve your ability but to be ready for a written paper you should practise past papers and attempt the worksheets in this book. Remember:

- Read all texts and extracts **thoroughly**, underlining as you go.
- Use your **dictionary**.
- Before you start the questions be sure and **read any notes provided**.
- After you have tried the various questions read the answers and **make a note of the language and phrases used**.
- Start making use of any **new phrases** you find as you progress through the book.
- Make sure you **consult the glossary** in the last chapter to help you attempt questions such as those on **literary devices**, tone, point of view, etc.
- When translating, it is the **meaning** of the sentence that counts. Translating word for word will lead to errors.

Tip 6: Exam day – cool, confident, careful

Select your preferred text carefully. Many students tend to go for the "Landeskunde" choice but quite often it is as difficult as the literary option. To help you with your choice look carefully at the extracts. Ask yourself:

- Which of the two texts is hardest to understand?

- Of the two topics which is more up my street? Which do I know more about?
- What are the comprehension and analysis questions like?
- Of the composition questions is there one I could write a really good answer to?
- How tricky is the translation? Before you go into the exam you should have a fair idea what your translating skills are like! Ask your teacher for advice about this.
- Which paper am I most confident of answering best?
- Have I a set plan of how much time I can give to each section? You should have a rough idea of how long to give to the various parts of your exam. In this respect it is highly important that you look at the number of marks each question carries with it. Although one particular question may be more difficult or simply need more time to answer you shouldn't spend ages answering a short, straightforward one that has 10 marks for the answer and very little time on one that carries 20, 30 or 50 marks. Take a good look at the marking scheme and plan accordingly!
- Make good use of your dictionary. Check your spelling!
- Stay cool, calm and collected – you have put in the work, the effort, the hours, it would be a pity not to show your teachers how much better you now are.

Finally, Good Luck!

Literature

Julius Caesar by William Shakespeare

The play opens with the public celebrating Caesar's victory in war over Pompey's sons. Caesar refuses a crown three times. Some men like Cassius and Flavius see Caesar's rise as a threat to the Republic. They warn Brutus that Caesar is becoming too powerful. Caesar is told by a wise man to beware of the Ides of March (March 15). Cassius continues to work on Brutus by sending him counterfeit messages, encouraging him to join the plot to murder Caesar. On the night before the Ides of March a fierce storm rages.

SCENE II. CAESAR's house.

Thunder and lightning. Enter CAESAR, in his night-gown.

CAESAR: Nor heaven nor earth have been at peace to-night:
Thrice hath Calphurnia in her sleep cried out,
'Help, ho! They murder Caesar!' Who's within?

Enter a Servant

SERVANT: My lord?

CAESAR: Go bid the priests do present sacrifice,
And bring me their opinions of success.

SERVANT: I will, my lord.

Exit

Enter CALPHURINA

CALPHURINA: What mean you, Caesar? Think you to walk forth?
You shall not stir out of your house to-day.

CAESAR: Caesar shall forth: the things that threaten'd me
Ne'er look'd but on my back; when they shall see
The face of Caesar, they are vanished.

CALPHURINA: Caesar, I never stood on ceremonies,

Yet now they fright me. There is one within,
Besides the things that we have heard and seen,
Recounts most horrid sights seen by the watch.
A lioness hath whelped in the streets;
And graves have yawn'd, and yielded up their dead;
Fierce fiery warriors fight upon the clouds,
In ranks and squadrons and right form of war,
Which drizzled blood upon the Capitol;
The noise of battle hurtled in the air,
Horses did neigh, and dying men did groan,
And ghosts did shriek and squeal about the streets.
O Caesar! these things are beyond all use,
And I do fear them.

CAESAR: What can be avoided
Whose end is purposed by the mighty gods?
Yet Caesar shall go forth; for these predictions
Are to the world in general, as to Caesar.

CALPHURINA: When beggars die, there are no comets seen;
The heavens themselves blaze forth the death of princes.

CAESAR: Cowards die many times before their deaths;
The valiant never taste of death but once.
Of all the wonders that I yet have heard,
It seems to me most strange that men should fear;
Seeing that death, a necessary end,
Will come, when it will come.
Re-enter Servant
What say the augurers?

SERVANT: They would not have you to stir forth to-day.
Plucking the entrails of an offering forth,
They could not find a heart within the beast.

CAESAR: The gods do this in shame of cowardice:
Caesar should be a beast without a heart,
If he should stay at home to-day for fear.
No, Caesar shall not: danger knows full well
That Caesar is more dangerous than he:
We are two lions litter'd in one day,

And I the elder and more terrible:
And Caesar shall go forth.

CALPHURINA: Alas, my lord,
Your wisdom is consumed in confidence.
Do not go forth to-day: call it my fear
That keeps you in the house, and not your own.
We'll send Mark Antony to the senate-house:
And he shall say you are not well to-day:
Let me, upon my knee, prevail in this.

CAESAR: Mark Antony shall say I am not well,
And, for thy humour, I will stay at home.
Enter DECIUS BRUTUS
Here's Decius Brutus, he shall tell them so.

DECIUS BRUTUS: Caesar, all hail! Good morrow, worthy Caesar:
I come to fetch you to the senate-house.

CAESAR: And you are come in very happy time,
To bear my greeting to the senators
And tell them that I will not come to-day:
Cannot, is false, and that I dare not, falser:
I will not come to-day: tell them so, Decius.

CALPHURINA: Say he is sick.

CAESAR: Shall Caesar send a lie?
Have I in conquest stretch'd mine arm so far,
To be afraid to tell greybeards the truth?
Decius, go tell them, Caesar will not come.

DECIUS BRUTUS: Most mighty Caesar, let me know some cause,
Lest I be laugh'd at when I tell them so.

CAESAR: The cause is in my will: I will not come;
That is enough to satisfy the senate.
But for your private satisfaction,
Because I love you, I will let you know:
Calphurnia here, my wife, stays me at home:
She dreamt to-night she saw my statua,
Which, like a fountain with a hundred spouts,
Did run pure blood: and many lusty Romans

Came smiling, and did bathe their hands in it:
And these does she apply for warnings, and portents,
And evils imminent; and on her knee
Hath begg'd that I will stay at home to-day.

DECIUS BRUTUS: This dream is all amiss interpreted;
It was a vision fair and fortunate:
Your statue spouting blood in many pipes,
In which so many smiling Romans bathed,
Signifies that from you great Rome shall suck
Reviving blood, and that great men shall press
For tinctures, stains, relics and cognisance.
This by Calphurnia's dream is signified.

CAESAR: And this way have you well expounded it.

DECIUS BRUTUS: I have, when you have heard what I can say:
And know it now: the senate have concluded
To give this day a crown to mighty Caesar.
If you shall send them word you will not come,
Their minds may change. Besides, it were a mock
Apt to be render'd, for some one to say
'Break up the senate till another time,
When Caesar's wife shall meet with better dreams.'
If Caesar hide himself, shall they not whisper
'Lo, Caesar is afraid'?
Pardon me, Caesar; for my dear, dear love
To our proceeding bids me tell you this;
And reason to my love is liable.

CAESAR: How foolish do your fears seem now, Calphurnia!
I am ashamed I did yield to them.
Give me my robe, for I will go. 897 words

From: Julius Caesar by William Shakespeare

Annotations
thrice (line 3): three times
stood on ceremonies (line 17): paid attention to omens
watch (line 20): guard
a lioness hath whelped (line 21): a lioness gave birth to
what can be avoided whose end is purposed by the mighty gods (line 32): whatever is going to happen will happen
augurers (line 43): priests
consumed in confidence (line 57): lost in, destroyed by, confidence
Decius Brutus (line 66): one of the men conspiring to kill Caesar. He is not to be confused with Brutus, one of the main characters in the play.
portents (line 90): signs
amiss (line 93): wrong(ly), incorrect(ly)
tinctures, stains, relics (line 99): all refer to medicines, ointments or healing remedies
expounded (line 101): explained it, put it into words.

Worksheet: *Julius Caesar*

Comprehension

1. Summarise the events of this scene in your own words (Minimum 150 words). Do not quote directly.
2. Identify two literary or stylistic devices in this scene and describe the use Shakespeare makes of them?
3. What role do the weather and omens play in this scene? Support your answer with examples.

Analysis

Choose *one* of the following tasks.
Write 200–300 words.

1. Describe and analyse the person Julius Caesar as shown in this film scene and in the extract from the play.

From: "Asterix – Sieg über Caesar" (orig.: Asterix et la surprise de Cesar), Frankreich 1985, Regie Gaetan Brizzi, Paul Brizzi; © JFV / Cinetext Bildarchiv

2. Contrast Calphurnia's attempts to persuade Caesar to stay at home with Decius efforts to get him to the Senate. Why does Decius succeed?

Composition

Choose *one* of the following tasks. Write a minimum of 200–300 words.

1. Select one person in history who you consider to have been a great leader. Outline the qualities that made the person a great leader and expand on the qualities that are necessary for someone to be a great leader? Under what circumstances would you consider it justified for conspirators to assassinate a political leader? If you wish you may refer to the play itself.
2. Imagine you are Calphurnia, Caesar's wife. Caesar has decided to go to the Senate despite the fact that you begged him not to. After he has gone you are very worried and cannot rest. Write a letter to a close friend in which you describe the situation as well as your fears and feelings. Your piece may also describe refer to Caesar as a husband, private person and political leader.

Key: *Julius Caesar*

Comprehension

1. *Summarise the events of this scene in your own words (minimum 150 words). Do not quote directly.*

Keep these points in mind before starting your answer:

- A good summary is **objective, complete** and **to the point**.
- What you are being asked to do here is to retell the main facts and ideas of the text – not to analyse it.
- **Use your own words** and do not quote directly from the text.
- Write the summary without long-winded introductions. Avoid beginnings such as "I am now going to summarise this short story by …"
- Use the simple present tense.
- When finished check your summary against the original text. Ask yourself if it is accurate. Does it read well? Check your punctuation and spelling.

The scene opens in Caesar's palace after a stormy night. Caesar informs us that Calphurnia has slept badly, having dreamt of his murder. Caesar sends a servant to tell the augurers to interpret the signs and tell him the result. Then Calphurnia tries to convince Caesar not to go to the senate. She describes the terrible nightmares she has had. The servant returns to inform Caesar that the augurers advise him to stay at home. Caesar pours scorn on this, saying he will go. Calphurnia asks him to give her anxiety for his safety as a reason why he cannot come. She suggests sending Mark Antony in his place and then bends down and begs her husband to stay at home. He agrees to do so. Decius arrives to accompany him to the Senate. When Caesar says he will not be going to the Senate, Decius asks what reason he should give. Caesar then explains Calphurnia's dreams and fears to Decius, telling him she saw blood pouring from Caesar's fountain. Decius says this is a positive sign that Rome will be revived by Caesar's blood. He tells Caesar that the senate wants to give Caesar an award. He also mentions that they may change their minds if Caesar does not come. This convinces Caesar to go to the Senate.

2. *Identify the important literary or stylistic devices in this scene and describe the use Shakespeare makes of them?*

It is not enough to simply write out a list of these devices. For such questions get into the habit of

- systematically reading through the text, **underlining** any devices you meet.
- choosing the ones you think the most important.
- describing the use made of them.
- asking yourself the following questions:
  What effect does the device have?
  Is it used to **improve the melody** of the piece? (e. g. alliteration)
  Does it draw the reader's attention to a contrast of some sort or to some aspect of a character's personality? (e. g. paradox, question)
  Does it tell the reader something that may happen in the future or that has happened in the past? (e. g. foreshadowing or flashback)

The most interesting device used in this scene is that of **foreshadowing**. Foreshadowing happens when the author gives hints about things which will later come to pass in the course of a story and that is exactly what Shakespeare does here. Calphurnia has nightmares and sees a statue of Caesar "which, like a fountain with a hundred spouts did run pure blood ..." This device is used to heighten the dramatic tension and it has the effect of giving the audience a glimpse of things to come.

The scene opens with an example of an **anaphora** "nor heaven nor earth, have been at peace to-night". This repetition emphasises just how stormy a night it is.

Likewise, **alliteration** is used throughout the scene by Shakespeare to achieve emphasis and melody in lines such as "have yawned and yielded up ..." (line 22), fierce, fiery warriors (line 23), "ghosts did shriek and squeal ..." (line 28), "your statue spouting blood" (line 95).

The **rhetorical question** "how foolish do your fears seem now" emphasises the scornful way in which Caesar speaks to his wife after he has decided to go to the Senate.

Another literary device one might refer to is the **paradox** Shakespeare presents the audience with in line 37 when he says "Cowards die many times before their death/The valiant never taste of death but once." This is a crucial statement, containing a fundamental truth, in a play which has the conflict of fate versus free will as one of its central themes.

3. *What role do the weather and omens play in this scene? Support your answer with examples.*

- To answer this properly read and **read again everything Caesar does or says.** Also consider what others do and say to him. Put yourself in the author's position.
- Choose your examples well. Your examples from this scene should prove a point. Do not, however, write an answer that is full of examples only. Start with an argument and support it.

Both the weather and the omens referred to in this scene are important in their own right. As Caesar wanders around in his night-gown, unable to sleep because his wife is having disturbing nightmares, there is thunder and lightning in the skies outside. These side effects make the moment more dramatic, exciting and frightening. The unrest inside the house is reflected in the weather itself. This is important because it tells the audience that the order of the universe has been disturbed, the Gods are in some way unhappy and something is either about to happen or has to happen which will restore order and calmness. The omens serve a similar purpose in terms of heightening the drama and tension in this scene though they have a second function also. Calphurnia tells Caesar she "never stood on cermonies" and never heeded the omens before but that this time her nightmares and the omens frighten her. She says that "a lioness hath whelped in the streets and graves have yawned and yielded up their dead". Then the news arrives that the priests "would not have you (Caesar) stir forth". Caesar brushes this warning off but the effect of the augurers' decision is to raise the dramatic tension. The omens are also used by Shakespeare to develop character. Indeed, we learn a great deal about the three main characters in this scene from the way they respond to Calphurnia's dreams and the omens. The Caesar we meet is unsure and superstitious. He cannot decide about them for himself but sends for the augurers to interpret the signs. This Julius Caesar is a man who believes in portents and dreams, a man who is indecisive and unable to make up his mind whether to go to the Senate. Decius is shown as clever and devious, while Calphurnia's feelings about these matters show her to be loyal and loving but at the end of the day she is not as clever as Decius.

Analysis

1. *Describe and analyse the person Julius Caesar as shown in this film scene and in the extract from the play. You may use information from the rest of the play if you wish.*

A detailed reading will show many sides to Caesar in this scene. Remember that to portray a character correctly you need to

- study his **behaviour**.
- carefully read what he says and how he reacts to others.
- note what **others say of/to him**? What reasons might they have for their statements?
- ask yourself has he **any unusual physical traits** or **personal habits**?
- include the **character's inner thoughts and feelings** if the author has made them clear to the reader.

When studying the scene from the film ask yourself:

- What is the cartoonist's aim?
- Where does the scene happen?
- Are contrasts or comparisons made?
- Is it a funny, sad or sarcastic shot?
- What differences exist between this shot and the scene from the play?

The two sides of Julius Caesar which we meet in this shot and in the extract are in many ways alike. The film shot shows Caesar as a cross old man with a big nose towering above a Roman who is bowing before mighty Julius. Caesar looks arrogant and pompous not to mention very vain. He is used to commanding people around, the way he does his wife in the extract. Like Act II Scene II this film shot also takes place indoors. The Roman looks as if he has come with a message for, or is taking orders from, Julius Caesar. In this respect he could be one of the servants from Act II Scene II. Although Caesar looks completely in control here there is a sense of weakness present in this shot. He towers above the Roman yet his legs are thin, his arms not one bit muscular. There are lines on his face. The point of view used by the cartoonist allows us to see Caesar high above the Roman, seemingly for more powerful than him, but in reality much weaker. This is quite similar to the way in which Shakespeare presents Caesar and Decius Brutus to us. Of course this film shot uses humour and sharp observation and presentation techniques to ridicule Caesar whereas William Shakespeare uses words and literary techniques to achieve his purpose. This film shot also limits itself to two particular characters, thus highlighting the differences between Caesar and the Roman, the cartoonist's overall aim. Act II Scene II is an important one in Shakespeare's overall portrayal of the character, Julius Caesar. As the scene opens we get a sight of Caesar, fresh from bed, where he could not sleep, and he strikes the reader as frightened. A worried man, this not the public leader we have known until now. Not only that but he is shown to believe in omens and immediately bids a servant go and ask the augurers to read the signs. All this happens when he is alone. Once his wife arrives he reverts to the public person, Julius Caesar, a man grown self-important thanks to his successes. Referring to the things that threatened him he says "when they shall see the face of Caesar; they are vanished". This Caesar, who later in the scene pours scorn upon his worried wife, is an arrogant man, accustomed to commanding people around. He is also a man who believes in the hand of fate as shown when he says "Death will come when it will come". Above all, he is a man who is susceptible to flattery. In lines 83–90 Decius fools Caesar by interpreting the dream as Caesar wants to hear it. Caesar is a vain man who likes being told he is great and good for Rome.

2. *Contrast Calphurnia's attempts to persuade Caesar to stay at home with Decius efforts to get him to the Senate. Why does Decius succeed?*

It is important to look in detail at the text in order to spot the differences. When asked to contrast two aspects of a text it is a good idea to make short written notes of how the two actually differ and build your answer around them. In this case that would mean:

CALPHURNIA:	DECIUS:
• genuinely worried	• superficially concerned
• direct approach	• clever use of flattery and pressure
• woman & partner	• man & political opponent

From the very start Calphurnia's approach to the situation reveals her to be a wife who is truly concerned for her husband's safety. Her tone is harsh and direct the moment she enters the room "What mean you Caesar? Think you to walk forth? You shall not stir out of your house today." She continues by trying to impress upon him how worried she is "I never stood on ceremonies yet now they fright me." She cites the things that frighten her and when Caesar will not come round to her wishes she asks him to say she is the reason why he cannot go to the Senate. Her approach, based on, and influenced by, a fear that is well-justified, is not as subtle as that displayed by Decius, who in winning Caesar round, keeps the plot to kill the emperor alive. His approach is a skilled and devious one. He greets Caesar cheerfully and calls him "worthy Caesar" and when Caesar announces he is not going Decius is quick to look for a reason so putting Caesar under pressure to justify his absence. This pressure he then increases by use of flattery, telling Caesar Calphurnia's dream means something else entirely. Caesar's blood would revive all Rome. Not satisfied with this he goes one step further and mentions the crown that awaits vain Caesar if he goes to the Senate. Caesar is by now already wavering "this way have you well expounded it ..." when Decius says the Senate will think Caesar not only a coward "Lo, Caesar is afraid!" but a man not able to go against his wife's, a woman's, wishes. The cleverness of Decius' approach and his dealing with what was an unexpected and difficult situation is shown by the fact that he gets Caesar to say "I am ashamed". Decius succeeds where Calphurnia fails because he pressurises and flatters the vain, macho side of Caesar in a highly skilful way. One has to say however that his task is easier than Calphurnia's, both because he is a man and as a person who knows what Caesar likes to hear.

Composition

1. *Select one person in history who you consider to have been <u>a great leader</u>. Outline the <u>qualities</u> that made the person a great leader and expand on the qualities that are necessary for someone <u>to be a great leader</u>? Under what <u>circumstances</u> would you consider it <u>justified for conspirators to assassinate</u> a <u>political</u> leader? If you wish you may refer to <u>the play</u> itself.*

When attempting a composition question it is important that

- you carefully read the question, **underlining the key words** (see above) as you do.
- you draw up a draft of your main ideas, examples and general thoughts to help you structure your essay well.

- you find a good introduction to gain the reader's attention. For such an introduction consider **a famous quotation** or **proverb** you know or a statistic you are aware of.
- you make use of linking sentences to give unity and flow to your essay.
- when finished you read your answer again, checking your **grammar, punctuation** and **spelling**.
- you ask yourself 'Have I answered the question?'
- you remember that when correcting the essay the teacher will concentrate on **language** and **content**.

"Cometh the hour, cometh the man" is a phrase often used with regard to the emergence of great leaders at difficult times in history. It conveys the idea that at certain crucial times, and in desperate or unusual situations great men – or women – step forward and display the qualities of leadership. The qualities that make a person a great leader are far from easy to define though they would include bravery, good timing, cool nerves, an ability to read people and situations correctly as well as an unshakeable self-confidence. Above all else a good leader has to be able to inspire people, to give them the feeling that he or she is the right person for the task in hand, the person who can show them the way out of current difficulties. Examples of men or women who fit the bill here would be Roosevelt, Indira Ghandi or Churchill.

The fact of the matter is that a great leader is born with certain qualities but he is also made, groomed if you like, by life itself, by his or her experiences. Churchill had developed into a tough and canny politician by the time Hitler marched into Poland but he had also become one of the outstanding orators of his century – of any century in fact – and this ability to use words is important for any great political leader. This was never more obvious than in Churchill's many wartime speeches held to bolster the nerve and resolve of the British people e. g. his "we shall never surrender" speech.

My choice as a great leader, however, would be Nelson Mandela. The qualities I see in his case are his unflinching bravery and determination in the face of cruelty and injustice, his patience and firmness, his humanity and readiness to listen to others and above all else his faith in the process of negotiation and reconciliation. It is this latter quality that makes him stand out for me – and this also contributed to a peaceful transition of power in South Africa in the 1990s. I would point out however that there are many other candidates I could have chosen – John Hume, Martin Luther King, to name but two outstanding names.

Finally, I believe it is rarely, if ever, justified to assassinate a political leader. It is certainly not something one can defend simply because – as in the play Julius Caesar – a man is getting too powerful. There have, of course, been many terrible despots in the history of the world. These were leaders who were very cruel. Often they violated human rights to such an extent when wiping out political opponents that had these leaders been assassinated, the action would have been defensible on humanitarian grounds. Examples of such men might be Joseph Stalin, Adolf Hitler and Idi Amin.

2. *Imagine you are Calphurnia, Caesar's wife. Caesar has decided to go to the Senate despite the fact that you begged him not to. After he has gone you are very worried and cannot rest. Write a letter to a close friend in which you describe the situation, your fears, and feelings. Your piece may also describe Caesar as a husband, private person and political leader.*

This is a creative writing exercise. When writing a letter these points are crucial to the success of your answer:

- Keep the reader in mind. Make the relationship of the writer to the recipient of the letter clear to your reader.
- Describe **the background** to your letter. This includes recent events and a description of the situation the writer finds himself/herself in. If suitable, use information from the text.
- Outline **the writer's emotional situation**. How does she or he feel?
- Do not forget the date, the location and the normal greetings used in a letter. The **formal aspects** of a letter are important in that if they are omitted points will be deducted.
- Finally, consider your conclusion carefully. Do you want a definite, all-revealing end to your piece or an open end which keeps the reader guessing? Note how the answer given here has an open end "these dreams do trouble me". The answer finishes with Calphurnia worried and fretting.

Rome, 15th March

My dearest Alexandra,

I hope my letter will find you in good spirits. Both Caesar and I enjoyed your visit to Rome. It is only a pity that I do not see more of you. Last night a great storm raged and it reminded me of the time when we, as small girls, hid together in your house. Our parents were away and the storm frightened us. Do you remember the candles we tried to light and how the winds kept blowing them out? It seems so long ago now.

I would have loved to have had you here these past few days. The news of Caesar's victories in battle will have reached you. He is triumphant. I have never known him so pleased, so convinced of his greatness. Everywhere he goes he is cheered by the people. This is by far the greatest moment of his glory. I should be happy for him but my heart will not let me. Last night I dreamt he was murdered by evil, jealous men, conspirators.

The other day a soothsayer warned him to beware of today, the Ides of March, and I too have tried, this very night, to convince him, because of my fears, my nightmares, to stay at home. Decius Brutus came a few hours ago and told him the senate wants to offer the great Julius Caesar a crown. How I dislike that fellow! There is something far too smooth and insincere about him. Vain fool that he is, Caesar laughed off all my warnings and has left for the Senate. Yet he was always like that – do you remember, the first time we saw him, how you told him he was a big head. He wanted to have nothing more to do with you though you have always been more pretty and beautiful than I am. His anger at that time told me how much he values praise and sweetness. Last night I was like you were that day – truthful and straight – and he scoffed at my dreams, rejected my advice.

All this makes me sad for I know him like no other person does. For the man that he is – uncertain and unsure – like a small child who needs someone to hold his hand. What would people say, those who think him a great leader, if they knew Caesar like I do? Yet I love him, Alexandra, as you know well, for he has been a good husband to me and I fear I will never see him again – this day or any other day. Pray for me, good friend, in my hour of despair. And write soon for my spirits need uplifting and these dreams do trouble me.

Your good friend,
Calphurnia

American Pastoral by Philip Roth

THE SWEDE

During the war years, when I was still a grade school boy, this was a magical name in our Newark neighborhood, even to adults just a generation removed from the city's old Prince Street ghetto and not yet so flawlessly Americanized as to be bowled over by the prowess of a high school athlete. The name was magical; so was the anomalous face. Of the few fair-complexioned Jewish students in our preponderantly Jewish public high school, none possessed anything remotely like the steep-jawed, insentient Viking mask of this blue-eyed blond born into our tribe as Seymour Irving Levov.

The Swede starred as end in football, center in basketball, and first baseman in baseball. Only the basketball team was ever any good – twice winning the city championship while he was its leading scorer – but as long as the Swede excelled, the fate of our sports teams didn't matter much to a student body whose elders, largely undereducated and overburdened, venerated academic achievement above all else. Physical aggression, even camouflaged by athletic uniforms and official rules and intended to do no harm to Jews, was not a traditional source of pleasure in our community – advanced degrees were. Nonetheless, through the Swede, the neighborhood entered into a fantasy about itself and about the world, the fantasy of sports fans everywhere: almost like Gentiles (as they imagined Gentiles), our families could forget the way things actually work and make an athletic performance the repository of all their hopes. Primarily, they could forget the war.

The elevation of Swede Levov into the household Apollo of the Weequahic Jews can best be explained, I think, by the war against the Germans and the Japanese and the fears that it fostered. With the Swede indomitable on the playing field, the meaningless surface of life provided a bizarre, delusionary kind of sustenance, the happy release into a Swedian innocence, for those who lived in dread of never seeing their sons or their brothers or their husbands again.

And how did this affect him – the glorification, the sanctification, of every hook shot he sank, every pass he leaped up and caught, every line drive he rifled for a double down the left-field line? Is this what made him that staid and stone-faced-boy? Or was the mature-seeming sobriety the outward manifestation of an arduous inward struggle to keep in check the narcissism that an entire community was ladling with love? The high school cheerleaders had a cheer for the Swede. Unlike the other cheers, meant to inspire the whole team or to galvanize the spectators, this was a rhythmic, foot-stomping tribute to the Swede alone, enthusiasm for his perfection undiluted and unabashed. The cheer rocked the gym at basketball games every time he took a rebound or scored a point, swept through our side of City Stadium at football games any time he gained a yard or intercepted a pass. Even at the sparsely attended home baseball games up at Irvington Park, where there was no cheerleading squad eagerly kneeling at the sidelines, you could hear it thinly chanted by the handful of Weequahic stalwarts in the wooden stands not only when the Swede came up to bat but when he made no more than a routine putout at first base. It was a cheer that consisted of eight syllables, three of them his name, and it went, Bah bah-*bah!* Bah bah bah ... bah-*bah!* and the tempo, at football games particularly, accelerated with each repetition until, at the peak of frenzied adoration, an explosion of skirt-billowing cartwheels was ecstatically discharged and the orange gym bloomers of ten sturdy little cheerleaders flickered like fireworks before our marvelling eyes ... and not for love of you or me but of the wonderful Swede. "Swede Levov! It rhymes with ... 'The Love'! ... Swede Levov! It rhymes with ... 'The Love'! ... Swede Levov! It rhymes with ... 'The Love'!"

Yes, everywhere he looked, people were in love with him. The candy store owners we boys pestered called the rest of us "Hey-you-no!" or "Kid-cut-it-out!"; him they called, respectfully, "Swede." Parents smiled and benignly addressed him as "Seymour." The chattering girls he passed on the street would ostentatiously swoon, and the bravest would holler after him, "Come back, come back, Levov of my life!" And he let it happen, walked about the neighborhood in possession of all that love, looking as though he didn't feel a thing. Contrary to whatever daydreams the rest of us may have had about the enhancing effect on ourselves of total, uncritical, idolatrous adulation, the love thrust upon the Swede seemed actually to *deprive* him of feeling. In this boy embraced as a symbol of hope by so many – as the embodiment of the strength, the resolve, the emboldened valor that would prevail to return our high school's servicemen home unscathed from Midway, Salerno, Cherbourg, the Solomons, the Aleutians, Tarawa – there appeared to be not a drop of wit or irony to interfere with his golden gift for responsibility.

But wit or irony is like a hitch in his swing for a kid like the Swede, irony being a human consolation and beside the point if you're getting your way as a god. Either there was a whole side to his personality that he was suppressing or that was as yet asleep or, more likely, there wasn't. His aloofness, his seeming passivity as the desired object of all this asexual lovemaking, made him appear, if not divine, a distinguished cut above the more primordial humanity of just about everybody else at the school. He was fettered to history, an *instrument* of history, esteemed with a passion that might never have been if he'd broken the Weequahic basketball record – by scoring twenty-seven points against Barringer – on a day other than the sad, sad day in 1942 when fifty-eight Flying Fortresses were shot down by Luftwaffe fighter planes, two fell victim to flak, and five more crashed after crossing the English coast on their way back from bombing Germany. 1000 words

Excerpt from AMERICAN PASTORAL by Philip Roth. Copyright © 1987 by Philip Roth.
Reprinted with permission of Houghton Mifflin Company. All rights reserved.

Annotations
Newark (line 2): A port town in New Jersey near New York.
insentient (line 7): lacking senses, inanimate
Midway (line 66): An atoll in the Central Pacific.
Salerno (line 66): A port in SW Italy.
Cherbourg (line 66): A port in NW France.
The Aleutians (line 67): A chain of volcanic islands beyond Alaska.
Tarawa (line 67): The capital of the Gilbert islands.
Flying Fortresses (lines 78/79): a type of plane

Worksheet: *American Pastoral*

Comprehension

1. In what kind of neighbourhood does Swede Levov grow up?
2. Why did people adore Swede Levov and what was so unusual about this?
3. What effect did this adoration of Levov have on him?

Analysis

Choose *one* of the following tasks. Write 200–300 words.

1. Evaluate this extract as the opening to a novel.
2. Explain the point of view the author uses here. Who is the narrator? From what you have read describe the narrator in the context of his role as a character in the novel and as a person.

Composition

Choose *one* of the following tasks. Write a minimum of 200–300 words.

1. Retell this story of growing up in Newark from Swede Levov's point of view.
2. You are a modern sporting hero such as David Beckham, Jan Ulrich, or someone real or fictitious of your own choosing. The pressure of life as a sporting hero has become too much for you and you decide to quit. A press conference to announce your decision is called. Write the statement you give in front of the cameras. Your statement should in particular refer to your sporting life but it should also contrast the life former heroes such as Swede Levov had with that of sportsmen nowadays.

photo: Liam Cleary

Key: *American Pastoral*

Comprehension

1. *In what kind of neighbourhood does Swede Levov grow up?*

The answer to this question is not one that jumps out at you. You will have to
- search carefully for the points to answer the question.
- ask yourself what the extract says about Newark.
- ask yourself what type of people live there.

Newark, the neighbourhood where the extract is set and where Swede and the narrator grow up, is primarily a Jewish area. It is located between the city centre and the suburbs. As such it is neither a ghetto, which one might expect of a city centre area, nor a typically American residential area. It is a place in between both of these types of neighbourhood but it is very similar to the rest of the city and to the rest of America in that it has a war on its mind – the Second World War. The other significant trait which Newark possessed and which deserves mention is the fact that academic degrees and third-level education are more important to the people living in the area than sport, sporting heroes or sporting achievements. Newark has, nevertheless, a ballpark, cheerleaders and, as we learn, one sporting hero. For most people war, work and study all come first. It does seem, however, like quite a nice place to grow up in and were it not for the absence of the sons and fathers gone off to war it would have been, generally-speaking, a normal place.

2. *Why did people adore Swede Levov and what was so unusual about this?*

In order to answer the second half of the question you have to
- look for any examples where people praised Levov and their reasons for doing so.
- consider the type of place Newark was and the type of person Swede Levov was.

People adored Swede Irving Levov for the simple reason that he had everything that anybody could want. He was goodlooking, physically robust and a superb athlete. All that Swede lacked was humour or irony. In addition to the attributes already referred to Swede was popular because he found a special place in the hearts and lives of all the local parents whose sons, brothers and husbands had gone off to war. Swede was the everyday replacement they found until the war was over. For the cheerleaders he was a local guy to adore and dream of falling in love with, and for the academic-minded Jews he was a hope of success in the sporting world. It was this last factor which made their adulation of Swede unusual. **Usually**, degrees were the key to fame, fortune or achievement in their eyes but that was not the case with Swede Levov. He was a sporting hero in a world which treasured degrees.

3. *What effect did this adoration of Levov have on him?*

- In particular ask yourself did Levov change because of all the adulation.
- Back up your answer with an example or two.

It seems as if all the adulation had little effect on Swede personally. One gets the impression from the extract that he let the whole thing wash over him and then continued doing whatever it was he had been doing. This did make him appear more distant, aloof and unresponsive than he already was. The narrator tells us that Levov did not have a sense of wit or irony which helped him to deal with the adulation. This made him somehow above everybody else, snobbish perhaps – though the author does not use this word. A major, yet secondary, effect of the adulation on Swede was to bind him forever in people's minds to the war in progress. As a person who was achieving sporting success at a time of war he came to represent a good and positive side to life especially at a time when the lives of local soldiers were threatened. This would have had an indirect rather than a direct effect on him. The overall effect of this adoration is very difficult to analyse because many of his traits were already there before he became a star.

Analysis

1. *Evaluate this extract as the opening to a novel.*

When evaluating a piece it is important to remember that among others you may have to

- carefully consider the material before you.
- make a judgement about the extract in question.
- come to a positive or negative decision about aspects of the material or the whole piece itself.

- say whether you personally like the piece e. g. poem, extract or style of writing and why.
- anticipate other people's arguments by coming up with points that refute a point of view you do not agree with.
- ask yourself, as in the case of this question, what it is you think makes the extract a success. Questions such as "Does the author, Philip Roth, succeed in catching the reader's attention?" must be answered if you are to evaluate this opening properly.

The extract used here consists of the first three pages of Philip Roth's acclaimed novel *American Pastoral*. As the opening to a substantial book it is assured, well-written and clearly the work of one of the leading novelists of our times. Philip Roth plunges the reader straight into the story of Swede Levov's life, its highs and lows, its successes and failures. The novel itself begins with two simple words "The Swede" and instantly the reader learns who it is that Philip Roth is talking about. **Not only that but** this short sentence has the effect not just of introducing us to Swede Levov but of plunging the reader into the life of Swede Levov, thus arousing our interest in the rest of the chapter. This interest once gained is not something the author is prepared to relinquish. He, through the voice of his narrator, Nathan Zuckerman, unravels bits of information over the next three pages in such a way that the reader has no option but to read on. He speaks of Levov's name, his sporting prowess, importance to the community, people's adulation of him and so on. Thus the reader is introduced to the novel's most central character and we are left with the feeling that we are in fact listening to someone speaking. Roth manages to do this by his ability to write a type of prose which, though packed with many difficult words, still sounds as if it could be spoken by the reader's next-door neighbour. Another technique used by Roth, and one which I especially like, is the withholding of information. Despite all we learn about Swede Levov there is still a great deal we do not know about him as the extract comes to a close. He is still an aloof figure and one about whom we know only so much. The urge to turn the page remains and that is the major achievement of this extract. There are some people who would criticise the patches of difficult prose which occasionally turn up in the extract but even if one does not fully understand every single word used here this, **in my opinion**, only serves to add to the mystique which surrounds Levov.

2. *Explain the point of view the author uses here. Who is the narrator? From what you have read describe the narrator in the context of his role as a character in the novel and as a person.*

When dealing with this question keep the following in mind:

- Point of View can be **first-person, third person objective, or omniscient**. Use examples from the scene itself to support your answer.
- Does the point of view alter how we assess the information received in any way?
- In this particular case you should try and find out what the **narrator's attitude** to Swede Levov is? Does he like, hate, admire him? Is he jealous of him?
- Do the main characters and the narrator meet? Is there any connection between them?
- What do we know of the narrator? Is he important or very insignificant? Do his views tell us anything?

As this book begins the reader learns that the narrator is a first person 'I' figure who later in the book turns out to Nathan Zuckerman, Philip Roth's longtime fictional tool. From the point of view used we are dealing here with a limited point of view situation, whereby the narrator knows enough to tell us Swede Levov's story though he will later need assistance from other characters in the book to complete the tale. All in all, he is a minor figure, particularly in the extract here, where we learn very little about him. What does come through however is that he, like so many other people in Newark, worshipped the ground that Levov stood on. Levov is a magical name to him. When he says "and how did this effect him – the glorification, the sanctification, of every hook shot he sank, every pass he leaped up and caught, every line ..." we can hear how the narrator admires Levov. As a person he sounds like an underachiever in sport and perhaps someone who was envious of Levov. He is also an astute observer and can recall a great deal of Levov's teenage years in Newark. Although he has a minor role to play it is nevertheless a crucial one in that Roth uses him to show Levov to the reader as the world saw him. This use of the narrator shows us exactly how skilled a writer Roth is.

Composition

1. *Retell this story of growing up in Newark from Swede Levov's point of view.*

When retelling a story from someone else's point of view you should

- **read the text again** from his point of view.
- **underline** every piece of information you intend to use.
- **place yourself in his or her shoes** and ask yourself questions:
  How would he or she have experienced these events or this period?
  How would he or she have felt at this point?
- If you know how others felt about him can you guess how he felt about them. In the case of Swede Levov it is important to try and guess what he felt about being a sporting hero.
- Try and introduce **a personal note** into your account e. g. his relationship with a brother or sister or friend.

Newark was okay, I suppose. Most of my memories are good ones. I grew up there and had the luck to be that little bit too young for the war. I was only average at school and spent most of my time in the ballpark. I played football, baseball and basketball and loved all of them. I suppose I got more out of the basketball as we won the city championship twice though I can't say I was better at one sport than the other. Life in Newark would have been dull if it hadn't been for sports. It's not exactly a place to write home about – most people dream of getting out into the world and becoming a teacher, a banker, a doctor or whatever. Not me – I lived for the sound of the crowd on match day. The fans, the songs, the cheerleaders. They were pretty girls though I never had time for a steady girlfriend what with all the training and playing. I suppose they all thought me great but it was lonely place in some ways – I didn't really get on with my parents and there weren't that many friends to play with. I remember seeing fathers and mothers and grandparents crying in one another's arms when news of a plane shot down and a son lost at sea reached our neck of the woods. What often amazed me was how worked up people could get at a game – men who couldn't walk not to mind run anymore would be so nice to me, supporting me at the game, even though they barely knew me. Only later I realised why. Sometimes I'd like to turn the clock back. These legs of mine aren't the fastest any more either. I had a brother too but he left Newark as soon as he could get out. Unlike me he wasn't much good at sports. It was probably hard for him that I was on every team around. The worst thing that I ever remember happening in Newark back then was the day four families in our neighbourhood lost a son. I remember coming home after a basketball match we'd won and seeing everybody crying. Normally, they'd be shouting over to me or asking me the result. They just looked at me with so much sadness in their eyes. It was a weird feeling.

2. *You are a modern sporting hero such as David Beckham, Jan Ulrich or someone real or fictitious of your own choosing. The pressure of life as a sporting hero has become too much for you and you decide to quit. A press conference to announce your decision is called. Write the statement you give in front of the cameras. Your statement should in particular refer to your sporting life but it should also contrast the life former heroes such as Swede Levov had with that of sportsmen nowadays.*

In order to write a good statement you must

- **structure it well** so that it develops logically from one point to another.
- choose a sporting hero and a sport that **you know something about**.
- refer to the person's **career and triumphs**, to the **pressures and problems** and, if possible, back each point up with an example?
- keep in mind you are telling the story of a person's career from his or her point of view.
- use **formal aspects** of a statement such as I'd like to thank you or Ladies and Gentlemen.

Good evening Ladies and Gentlemen,
"**I'd like to thank you** all for coming here at such short notice. I see many familiar faces among the journalists before me here tonight, people I've known all my sporting life. Football has often been good to me. I started playing in my home town and went to Nottingham Forest at the age of 15. I've won every honour there is to be won at club level. Most of you would choose the night we beat Bayern Munich as the highpoint of my life as a footballer yet the Premiership titles I won were just as important to me. Particularly the ones where Arsenal came second. (Laughter).
Being a sportsman nowadays is not easy. The physical demands of playing at the highest level leave many players such as myself with long-term injuries and pain for the rest of their lives. In my case I have had more operations than most of you've had dinners. As a result of this I have decided to announce my retirement from the game. The doctors here say that if I do not stop playing I may live to regret it. I have however reached the decision

because of other factors as well. **The fact of the matter is that** I get to spend very little time with my family and this has become a problem. When the club plays in Newcastle on Saturday, Kiev on Tuesday and London on the following Saturday my family never gets to see me. Likewise, the appointments I have to keep to promote the products of our sponsors add to the already heavy load I carry. This decision may seem strange to all my fans, who I would personally like to thank for their support, but fame is a double-edged sword. It undoubtedly brings financial reward, it also brings hard work and photographers taking photos of my wife when we are supposed to be splitting up, as well as journalists to the door when we are having a private birthday party. Likewise, I end up in court defending my name when a woman claims I hit her even though I did not. Long ago sportsmen earned less but they also had a private life, less travelling and more time for themselves. That, unfortunately, is no longer the case. They did, of course, not have the back-up system we enjoy in terms of trainers and physios and agents but sometimes I think I was born thirty or forty years too late.

For me the time is now right to stop playing. I thank everyone at my club, my fans and fellow professionals for the good sides of life as a professional footballer. Thank you very much.

War Photographer by Carol Ann Duffy

In his darkroom he is finally alone
with spools of suffering set out in ordered rows.
The only light is red and softly glows,
as though this were a church and he
a priest preparing to intone a Mass.
Belfast. Beirut. Phnom Penh. All flesh is grass.

He has a job to do. Solutions slop in trays
beneath his hands which did not tremble then
though seem to now. Rural England. Home again
to ordinary pain which simple weather can dispel,
to fields which don't explode beneath the feet
of running children in a nightmare heat.

Something is happening. A stranger's
features faintly start to twist before his eyes,
a half-formed ghost. He remembers the cries
of this man's wife, how he sought approval
without words to do what someone must
and how the blood stained into foreign dust.

A hundred agonies in black-and-white
from which his editor will pick out five or six
for Sunday's supplement. The reader's eyeballs prick
with tears between the bath and pre-lunch beers.
From the aeroplane he stares impassively at where
he earns his living and they do not care.

© Carol Ann Duffy
War Photographer is taken from Standing Female Nude
by Carol Ann Duffy, Anvil Press Poetry, 1985

Worksheet: *War Photographer*

Comprehension

1. What is meant by the line "spools of suffering set out in ordered rows"?
2. Some of the photographs will be chosen for printing in the newspaper's Sunday supplement. What bothers the photographer about this and the effects they will have on readers?
3. What, in your opinion, is the main theme of this poem? What was Carol Ann Duffy primarily setting out to do when she wrote this poem?

Analysis

Choose *one* of the following tasks. Write 200–300 words.

1. Analyse the function of religion and religious images in this poem.
2. Comment on the structure of the poem.

Composition

Choose *one* of the following tasks. Write a minimum of 200–300 words.

1. Imagine you are the war photographer who took this shot. Two years afterwards you have returned home to your native city and are thinking about this photograph, the day in question and your life now. Write a creative piece describing how you felt on that day, the events that happened and how you are coming to terms with your life away from war zones.

© David C. Turnley, Corbis Images

2. You are a former war photographer speaking to journalists after the opening of your first photographic exhibition in over ten years. In the course of your conversation you are asked the question "Are you not ashamed of the fact that you are famous, rich and alive whereas many of your subjects are either forgotten, still living in poverty, or dead?" Write an answer to this question.

Key: *War Photographer*

Comprehension

1. *What is meant by the line "spools of suffering set out in ordered rows"?*

To people experienced in photography this is a fairly straightforward question. It may help to ask yourself how a photographer works in a non-digital darkroom.

The spools in question here refer to the material that a photographer takes out of his film canisters once he opens and develops a film in the dark room. Once the developing process has been completed he is left with the negatives from which he will get a positive print or photograph. Most photographers initially set out their negatives in rows and make what is known as a contact print in which each photo on the film can be seen side by side at a smaller size. This contact print is used to decide which photos to enlarge. In the case of the war photographer in this poem the photographs he shot were of people suffering in a war situation. Hence the spools set out in rows are the negatives lined up side by side on a worktable or on printing paper. They are a photographic record of the terrible war situation and the people's suffering as the photographer documented it.

2. *Some of the photographs will be chosen for printing in the newspaper's Sunday supplement. What bothers the photographer about this and the effects they will have on readers?*

In answering this question you are expected to

- look at the issue from the photographer's point of view.
- identify the photographer's feelings about how the readers feel and react on seeing his work.
- elaborate on this using quotes from the poem to support what you say.

The first thing that bothers the photographer is that **he is fully aware** of the fact that, of the "hundred agonies in black-and-white" which he shot, his editor "will pick out five or six" and use them for the Sunday newspaper supplement. This is something he has to live with but for him it means that another person will edit his work and print what the newspaper wants to print rather than what he himself might choose to print. It cannot tell the whole story of his experience and this is hard to accept. Secondly, there is a certain feeling that although "the reader's eyeballs prick with tears" this emotion is somewhat false in that the reader does not go and try and help the people concerned but continues with his "bath and pre-lunch beers." In the photographer's mind there is always the feeling that the readers may not care. While the photographer is probably thrilled to have a contract and work he cannot help feeling a great deal of regret about the fact that the people who see his work do not take the plight of the war torn countries seriously.

3. *What, in your opinion, is the main theme of this poem? What was Carol Ann Duffy primarily setting out to do when she wrote this poem?*

A question about the main theme of a poem requires you to say, in your own words

- what the subject of the poem is.
- what the poet's thoughts and feelings on this matter are.
- how the poet expresses this in the course of writing the poem.

The main theme of this poem is the dilemma of someone who has to do an unpleasant job. In this case the subject is a war photographer and he is seen by the poet as a recorder of truth. **The poet sees** the photographer as a person who has to go to a foreign country and face terrible scenes in the course of his work. This predicament, and the pain he experiences when he returns to "spools of suffering" in his darkroom, reminds the poet of mass and a church with the photographer being somewhat like the priest. In the darkroom the photographer cannot escape the agony of the people he saw dying before his very eyes. The faces appear on paper and he cannot get away from them. The dilemma of the photographer is made more poignant by the introduction of a troubled conscience in verse four. **Here the poet examines** the extent to which the photographer ponders the value of his job. Doubts are raised in his mind about the value of his job if all it does is horrify people who are having a few beers and will do nothing else about the agony they see in their newspaper. Carol Ann Duffy has set out to place the job of a war photographer under the loupe. But **the poet also draws attention to** the contrast between "rural England" and scenes of war, between first-hand experience and sanitised versions in colour supplements. She notes how the photographer moves between two worlds but belongs wholly to neither.

Analysis

1. *Analyse the function of religion and religious images in this poem.*

To complete this question successfully it is important

- to ask yourself what the **similarities** are between the two men, the priest and the photographer
- to underline the **differences** between the two men.
- to point out why the poet might want to include religion in the poem.
- to be able to say that the term "All flesh is grass" is of religious origin.

Most of the material of a religious nature in this poem comes when the poet writes "The only light is red and softly glows, as though this were a church and he a priest preparing to intone a Mass." In **doing so the poet draws a comparison between** the priest and the photographer. Both men work in the presence of a red light and both men have a message to pass on. In the case of the photographer this message is one designed to tell the truth of what is happening in war-torn countries. The horror and the pain of death in a war situation compare and contrast well with Mass as a celebration of death. Both men are, in their own ways, trying to achieve something similar. There are differences, of course. The photographer has a larger audience and an immediately more shocking message. He has concrete evidence for his readers and no leap of faith or belief is needed. The priest and mass as a ceremony is an ideal vehicle for the poet as she examines issues such as truth and the need for goodness in the world. Later she points at the horror of death with a semi-religious image when she says "the blood stained into foreign dust". The function of religion is to allow for comparison and contrast in the poem and to emphasise the importance of the photographer, his work and his message. **One last point to refer to is** the line "All flesh is grass." This, too, has a religious theme within it both in the way it sounds as we read the poem and its meaning. Using this religious quotation, the poet reminds the reader that life is being wasted, lives are fragile things, people are dying and being buried all over the world. This quote from Isaiah serves the poet's purpose well, reminding the reader that the photographer, too, will perish either on the battlefield or elsewhere.

2. *Comment on the structure of the poem.*

When attempting such a question please remember that you may have to
- refer to **the number of stanzas** in the poem.
- point out **the number of lines** in each stanza.
- draw attention to **the rhyme scheme** used by the poet.
- say what function **the structure** of the poem has.

This poem is made up of four conventional stanzas. Each stanza contains six lines, a fact which gives the poem a solid, unified and well-structured look. The rhyme scheme used is one of rhymed iambic lines. An example of this would be "to fields which don't explode beneath the feet of running children in a nightmare heat." Each stanza ends with a couplet and one gets the impression that the poet does this to conclude an argument, to emphasise a point: e. g. "All flesh is grass", "stained into foreign dust", "they do not care." The stanzas having a firm and definite structure allows the poem to move from a series of observations to a clear conclusion. One of the most interesting aspects of the structure of the poem is the use the poet makes of syntax, in particular of short lines. "Rural England, All flesh is grass. Belfast. Beirut. Phnom Penh. Something is happening" all force the reader to consider what the poet is saying. The meaning of such short sentences is very clear, the message is hammered home. Never is this more obvious than when Carol Ann Duffy writes "He has a job to do". Short and straight to the point. The importance of the structure of this poem should not be overlooked. It is the adherence to a definite layout which gives the poem, and in particular the message of the poem, its strength, its punch, ending appropriately with the statement "they do not care".

Composition

1. *Imagine you are the war photographer who took this shot. Two years afterwards you have returned home to your native city and are thinking about this photograph, the day in question and your life now. Write a creative piece describing how you felt on that day, the events that happened and how you are coming to terms with your life away from war zones.*

To answer this properly you must
- place yourself in the photographer's shoes.
- add in atmosphere by means of sights, smells, inner thoughts and feelings.

New York in winter can be a depressing, grim place. As I write, one of the worst snowstorms on record is battering the streets and sidewalks of my native city. It's a far cry from the place where I took this shot. South Africa, another day at work, and I had no idea I was about to take my best, my favourite shot as a war photographer. God, how young and fresh and unfrightened I felt! I saw the gunman run forward, saw my friends beyond him again, and click! How thrilling that was! Back in the good old days when magazines paid decent money and there were only a few of us who could really say we were war photographers. Nowadays editors couldn't care less. Digital is on the way in, guys like myself on the way out. After my first job – covering the Tet offensive in Vietnam – I was hooked and have been ever since then. I've seen action in places like Nyerubuye and Afghanistan. What I never forget is the smell of a place where I took a shot – like the day I took this one – Sweat, sticky sweat on my camera body, in my armpits, on his brow as he ran past, and the smell of burning rubber. Or in Rwanda – the stench of burning bodies, corpses, bones. Was I afraid? Never. Only lonely. Fear is an isolating experience. You are alone with your camera and fate. On July 12, 1993 four of my friends were shot by a mob in Mogadishu. I left on the last plane out of there the night before. Now I'm home and I hate the cold, the silence of the phone. I remember a time when a guy ... hey hang on a minute ... I'm dying for a drink. Just one.

2. *You are a former war photographer speaking to journalists after the opening of your first photographic exhibition in over ten years. In the course of your conversation you are asked the question "Are you not ashamed of the fact that you are famous, rich and alive whereas many of your subjects are either forgotten, still living in poverty, or dead?" Write an answer to this question.*

To attempt this question you should feel able to
- place yourself in the shoes of the photographer.
- remember that this is a strong accusation and needs to be answered well.
- include details to flesh out your answer.

Well, that's a serious accusation you are making. Basically, **if I understand you correctly**, what you are saying is that I have used my subjects for my own gain. I reject that, of course, but it is not the first time someone has said that to me. Some newspapers and magazines do have photographers working for them who invade the lives of their subjects and get well paid for doing so. Sometimes this can lead to tragedy. The case of Princess Diana **comes to mind**. There is a sense, of course, in which every photographer is making use of his subject. I admit that. I am, however, not as rich or famous as your question makes me out to be and I am not ashamed of the fact that I have survived. **I am very grateful** to be alive and though I no longer cover wars I still struggle with the meaning of all my experiences. As a friend of mine once wrote "You sleep with the dead, you cradle the dead, you live with the living who become the dead. Seeing, looking at what others cannot bear to see, is what my life as a war reporter is all about." I think I can be proud of my role and my work. There were many situations which as a war photographer I saw and which as a person I could not accept. I have never been able to switch off my feelings, nor do I think it would be right to do so. But nor was there much I could have done to save the people I saw killed in battle. There has always been a sense of guilt on returning to my home, to the comfort I enjoy, to the peace of it all. **It is unfair** that I am alive and they are dead, that I am able to choose my destiny and they are not. I wish I could do more in actual terms to help such people in their plight. But I can't. The war photographer is limited by the nature of his job. I do like to think that my photos and the photos of other war photographers have helped to end wars. I therefore feel no shame but a certain guilt perhaps when I, as a citizen and voter, think of the damage my country has done, the damage other nations have inflicted on helpless peoples. Sometimes I see the faces and know they are no longer alive and that disturbs me very much. I'm not sure if that fully answers your question but perhaps you'll stop and think before you pose it again.

Indian Killer by Sherman Alexie

John attended St. Francis Catholic School from the very beginning. His shoes always black topsiders polished clean. His black hair very short, nearly a crew cut, just like every other boy in school. He was the only Indian in the school, but he had friends, handsome white boys. And John had danced with a few pretty white girls in high school. Mary, Margaret, Stephanie. He had fumbled with their underwear in the back seats of cars. John knew their smell, a combination of perfume, baby powder, sweat, and sex. A clean smell on one level, a darker odor beneath. Their breasts were small and perfect. John was always uncomfortable during his time with the girls, and he was never sorry when it was over. He was impatient with them, unsure of their motives, and vaguely insulting. The girls expected it. It was high school and boys were supposed to act that way. The girls assumed the boys were much more complicated than they actually were. Inside, John knew that he was more simple and shallow than other boys, and less than real.

"What are you thinking?" the girls always asked John. But John knew the girls really wanted to tell him what they were thinking. John's thoughts were merely starting points for the girls to talk about mothers and fathers, girlfriends, ex-boyfriends, pets, clothes, and a thousand other details. John felt insignificant at those times and retreated into a small place inside of himself, until the girls confused his painful silence with rapt interest.

The girls' fathers were always uncomfortable when they first met John, and grew more irritated as he continued to date Mary, Margaret, or Stephanie. The relationships began and ended quickly. A dance or two, a movie, a hamburger, a few hours in a friend's basement with generic rock music playing softly on the radio, cold fingers on warm skin.

"I just don't think it's working out," she'd tell John, who understood. He could almost hear the conversations that had taken place.

"Hon," a father would say to his daughter. "What was that boy's name?"

"Which boy, daddy?"

"That dark one."

"Oh, you mean John. Isn't he cute?"

"Yes, he seems like a very nice young man. You say he's at St. Francis? Is he a scholarship student?"

"I don't know. I don't think so. Does it matter?"

"Well, no. I'm just curious, hon. By the way, what is he? I mean, where does he come from?"

"He's Indian, daddy."

"From India? He's a foreigner?"

"No, daddy, he's Indian from here. You know, American Indian. Like bows and arrows and stuff. Except he's not like that. His parents are white."

"I don't understand."

"Daddy, he's adopted."

"Oh. Are you going to see him again?"

"I hope so. Why?"

"Well, you know. I just think. Well, adopted kids have so many problems adjusting to things, you know. I've read about it. They have self-esteem problems. I just think, I mean, don't you think you should find somebody more appropriate?"

The door would shut with a loud and insistent click. Mary, Margaret, or Stephanie would come to school the next day and give John the news. The daughters would never mention their fathers. Of course, there were a few white girls who dated John precisely because they wanted to bring home a dark boy. Through all of it, John repeatedly promised himself he would never be angry. He didn't want to be angry. He wanted to be a real person. He wanted to control his emotions, so he would often swallow his anger. Once or twice a week, he felt the need to run and hide. In the middle of a math class or a history exam, he would get a bathroom pass and quickly leave the classroom. His teachers were always willing to give him a little slack. They knew he was adopted, an Indian orphan, and was leading a difficult life. His teachers gave him every opportunity and he responded well. If John happened to be a little fragile, well, that was perfectly understandable, considering his people's history. All that alcoholism and poverty, the lack of God in their lives. In the bathroom, John would lock himself inside a stall and fight against his anger. He'd bite his tongue, his lips, until sometimes they would bleed. He would hold himself tightly and feel his arms, legs, and lower back shake with the effort. His eyes would be shut. He'd grind his teeth. One minute, two, five, and he would be fine. He would flush the toilet to make his visit seem normal, slowly wash his hands and return to the classroom. His struggles with his anger increased in intensity and frequency until he was visiting the bathroom on a daily basis during his senior year. But nobody noticed. In truth, nobody mentioned any strange behaviour they may have seen. John was a trailblazer, a nice trophy for St. Francis, a successfully integrated Indian boy. 827 words

© Sherman Alexie 1996. Used by permission ot Grove/Atlantic, Inc.

Worksheet: *Indian Killer*

Comprehension

1. Describe John's situation at St Francis school as he experienced it?
2. Why was John of interest to the many girls he dated?
3. What exactly do you think it was that caused John to lock himself in a bathroom stall and fight against his anger?

Analysis

Choose *one* of the following tasks. Write 200–300 words.

1. Comment on the function and quality of the part of the text from line 26 to line 48.
2. Study the painting you see here and answer the following questions: Describe what you see in your own words and contrast the picture we get of Indians here to that presented to us in the extract.

George Catlin, © akg, Berlin

Composition

Choose *one* of the following tasks. Write a minimum of 200–300 words.

1. The attitudes of white Americans towards Indians has always been at very best ambivalent.
   Discuss. You may refer to the text if you wish.
2. Does literature have the power to change society?
   Write an essay on the above question.

Key: *Indian Killer*

Comprehension

1. *Describe what the reader learns about John's origins, his appearance and position at school.*

Ask yourself the following questions:
- What do people say about John?
- How is he described?
- How do people treat John e. g. girlfriends, fathers, teachers?

In the course of reading this text we learn that John is an adopted American Indian, an orphan whose parents had died. We also find out that he is a young man with short black hair so short it could almost be called a crew cut. He wore clean shoes, was dark-skinned and "cute". His position at school is somewhat harder to describe. **On the one hand** he was a typical schoolboy – he dressed and looked like most of his classmates – except of course for the colour of his skin. He did many of the things his mates did – dated girls, went to the movies, went for hamburgers and so on. He had many handsome white friends but at the end of the day John was the only Indian at the school and this set him apart. It did so particularly in the eyes of his teachers. Most of them took extra pity on him because of his background. They treated him more leniently that the others in their classes. In the eyes of his teachers John was well-integrated. At a superficial level then everything seemed okay. As we learn in the text extract however John had major problems.

2. *Why was John of interest to the many girls he dated?*

John was of interest to the girls he dated for a number of different reasons. **First of all**, he would have been physically attractive to them. He was a dance partner for some of them and later got to know them physically in the backs of cars and in apartments. This was a natural attraction even if he had difficulties with it. As far as the girls were concerned he was a high school boy of their age and very interesting. He was, however, interesting because he was prepared to listen to them. The girls liked talking to him because he didn't interrupt all the time and gave them a chance to speak their mind. **Finally**, he was particularly interesting for those girls who wanted to annoy their fathers by bringing home a dark-skinned boy. For such girls he was a weapon in a war and they used him gladly.

3. *What exactly do you think it was that caused John to lock himself in a bathroom stall and fight against his anger?*

The important word in this question is the word exactly. You must

- reveal the exact reason. To do this you will have to come to a conclusion afer reading the full text.
- concentrate on his position among and with white people.

This question needs a careful answer in that there may have been a number of reasons. A major part of the problem was John's experience of girls and the relationships, usually very brief and unsatisfactory, which he had with them. The rejection he experienced at their hands – it was always the girls who ended the relationship – made him a bitter and angry boy. Likewise their fathers' reactions to him was unhelpful and a cause of his misery. But **another factor should not be overlooked** in this. John's experience of teachers was also negative. Instead of treating him like any other boy they poured pity, hurtful, useless pity on him. At a time when he needed integration and a helping hand they convinced themselves that he was well-integrated and were fooled by their own cliched understanding of what a difficult life he had. Though they noticed he was starting to act strangely they just looked on. It was white people's attitudes to John that drove him to the loneliness of the bathroom stall.

Analysis

1. *Comment on the function and quality of the part of the text from line 26 to line 48.*

You are being asked about two aspects of the part of the text. Ask yourself:

- How is this piece different to the rest of the extract?
- Why is this piece written this way?
- What does the reader learn about John and the white people he knew?
- How good a piece of writing is this? Why is it good, bad, well-written, unnatural?

When he was writing this book, the author Sherman Alexie wanted to address the problem of white people's attitudes to Indians. In this extract he chooses a definite technique to do so. For the most part Alexie uses detailed and structured prose to describe John's experiences at St Francis Catholic school. When it comes to giving the reader an idea of the impact he made on white people's lives however, Alexie chooses to present us with a dialogue that takes place between a nameless father and daughter. The reader is thus given a fly on the wall view of how people spoke about John and what they thought of him. The father's curiosity and disapproval of his daughter's relationship with John and the daughter's mainly positive attitude both come out in the discussion. John is referred to by the father as "That dark one" and is inappropriate. The girl thinks he's cute and hopes to see him again. But she does not and ends the relationship. **The function of the dialogue** is to show their attitudes to John and the consequences of the parent's blindness. Inevitably, the fathers force the daughters not to see a "bow-and-arrows" Indian again. Alexie smoothly highlights John's isolation, his loneliness and the way in which white people hurt him, thus showing his technical ability as a writer of modern prose. The snappy end to this piece "The door would shut with a loud and insistent click" not only emphasises the hurt John feels, as if something were breaking inside him, but it also allows for a smooth return to the style of writing of the previous pages.

2. *Study the painting you see here and answer the following questions: Describe what you see in your own words and contrast the picture we get of Indians here to that presented to us in the extract.*

In this case you should
- use your own description of the picture.
- ask yourself how it differs from the extract.

This is a painting which depicts Indians taking part in a buffalo hunt. The scene occurs in open country and the landscape is very striking. In the foreground, to the right of the picture, an Indian bearing a bow and arrow is in the process of killing a buffalo. He is scantly clad and has long black hair. A second Indian can be seen astride a buffalo and horse and he too has a bow in his hand. In the very forefront of the picture a horse and a buffalo have fallen to the ground in a most dramatic way. Way off in the distance a third Indian is chasing buffalo up a hill.
The picture presented to us here by artist George Catlin is very dramatic but at the same time it is a romantic one. It is a bow and arrow portrait of Indians chasing buffalo. It is also a picture drawn by a non-Indian, a white man viewing Indians at work. The picture emphasizes everything we think of when Indians come into our minds; bows and arrows, savages, skilled horsemen, the buffalo hunt, the athletic, fearless hunters of the Great Plains and so on. Within this portrait other themes exist beneath the actual surface drawing; the beauty of the American landscape, the romantic 19th century notion of the Indians as a noble savage destined to die out. Catlin's picture could not be more different to the picture we get in Indian Killer. The Indian we meet is lonely, angry and isolated. He is experiencing personal difficulties in his relationships with white people. Alexie's picture is one drawn by an Indian and is a far deeper and more complicated one as a result. Catlin's drawing is done for white people – to show them how the Indians worked, to provide a record of a people soon to die out. Of the two portraits Alexie's shows a deep understanding of the plight of the Indians today, Catlin's is done with affection but is limited by being part of the romantic blinkered view of Indians that existed in the 19th century.

Composition

1. *The attitudes of white Americans towards Indians has always been at very best ambivalent.*
   Discuss. You may refer to the text if you wish.

The points to consider here are:

- Have the attitudes been ambivalent and if so how?
- Have they changed in any way over the years?
- Can you think of an example of someone who typifies a certain attitude toward the Indians.
- What writers or politicians have sought to change things?

Native Americans have long been a thorn in the conscience of white Americans. There was a time in fact when most white people fully believed the thesis that the only good Indian is a dead Indian. Indeed some still hold on to such John-Wayne, gun and holster beliefs. However, it is also true to say that attitudes toward the Indians in the USA have undergone considerable change and this is a point that I will come to later. What are the attitudes of white Americans towards Indians and how ambivalent are they? In the eyes of many white Americans, Indians threaten the WASP culture they so treasure. Indians are seen in a negative light; they take low paid jobs, live in dirty, unhealthy circumstances, are only fit for life on the reservation, drink and gamble too much and are a burden on the taxpayer. Such people also believe that Indians increase the rate of crime and fuel racial problems.
Yet many Americans see their country as a land of liberty and acknowledge the right of an Indian to freedom and see acceptance of Indians as proof that human equality is alive and well in the USA. Indeed, people are capable of showing both these types of attitudes and therein lies the ambivalence. This comes across in the text through the attitudes of the teachers to John. He is to be pitied, he is to be treated differently and we should be nice to him even if, or rather because, he is not as good as we are. Attitudes towards Indians do of course vary from person to person, from class to class and from background to background. It is necessary to mention the change that has occurred in people's general view of the treatment of the Indians down through the years. The work of historians such as Dee Brown, or the authors Louise Edrich or Sherman Alexie has encouraged a revision of the judgement history has passed on this terrible episode in US life. Both the importance of the role of Native Americans in US history and the mass injustice

committed against a proud people have been acknowledged to a far greater degree in recent times. It is to be hoped that this will continue and that ambivalence in attitudes will be further reduced to allow Native Americans to be seen more in an ordinary and normal light.

2. *Does literature have the power to change society?*
Write an essay on the above question.

If you decide to do this question it is important that:
- You can refer to a number of books or authors who have changed society.
- You can discuss how and why books change the world we live in.
- You are able to include examples or sayings of one sort another to back up your point.

In my humble opinion there is no doubt but that literature does have the power to change society. **One only has to consider** the impact books such as The Bible, Das Kapital, The Communist Manifesto and The Playboy of the Western World to know that **from time to time** certain works of literature are published which have a huge impact on the world as we know it. When Synge wrote The Playboy it lead to riots in Dublin and questions were released into the public domain which would be part and parcel of the whole political change that took place in Ireland in the following decades. The impact of literature is not always good. One only has to consider other examples such as Mein Kampf to realise the negative potential literature has. As the reader will have noticed most of the examples quoted so far have to do with religion and politics. Does that mean that it is only in this area that literature can have an impact on society?
Think about prison inmates for a moment. This is a social area where literature can bring about great change. Prisoners are frequently given books to read in an attempt to improve them as people. Reading consists of a direct and immediate engagement with language. Discussing what we read intensifies this engagement, giving us an increased sense of authority and self-confidence. As we build language skills, we build life skills. We learn our place within the world of language. We become productive citizens. Good literature allows criminal offenders to feel personal experiences and encourages them to reflect on those experiences. Literature can teach criminal offenders that they are not alone and assist offenders in understanding that there are many ways of thinking about a person or an event. More

importantly, perhaps, it teaches them that they have the ability to choose their actions.

The power of literature to bring about change is closely linked to the power of language too. When politicians use language to convince people of their position and to win support they are doing something very similar to what authors do. Anybody reading Indian Killer by Sherman Alexie would come away with a new understanding of the problems facing Indians in America today. The pen, it is said, is mightier than the sword. I'm not sure if I would go that far but there is no doubt that literature has the power to change society.

How to be Good by Nick Hornby

I come home the next night to the sound of trouble; even as I'm putting the key in the lock I can hear Tom shouting and Molly crying.

'What's going on?' David and the kids are sitting around the kitchen table, David at the head, Molly to his left, Tom to his right. The table has been cleared of its usual detritus – post, old newspapers, small plastic models found in cereal packets – apparently in an attempt to create the atmosphere of a conference.

'He's given my computer away,' says Tom. Tom doesn't often cry, but his eyes are glistening, either with fury or tears, it's hard to tell.

'And now I've got to share mine,' says Molly, whose ability to cry has never been in any doubt, and who now looks as though she has been mourning the deaths of her entire family in a car crash.

'We didn't need two,' says David, 'Two is ... Not obscene, exactly. But certainly greedy. They're never on the things at the same time.

'So you just gave one away. Without consulting them. Or me.'

'I felt that consultation would have been pointless.'

'You mean that they wouldn't have wanted you to do it?'

'They maybe wouldn't have understood why I wanted to.'

It was David, of course, who insisted on the kids having a computer each for Christmas last year. I had wanted them to share, not because I'm mean, but because I was beginning to worry about spoiling them, and the sight of these two enormous boxes beside the tree (they wouldn't fit under it) did nothing to ease my queasiness. This wasn't the kind of parent I wanted to be, I remember thinking, as Tom and Molly attacked the acres of wrapping paper with a violence that repelled me; David saw the look on my face and whispered to me that I was a typical joyless liberal, the sort of person who would deny their kids everything and themselves nothing. And here I am six months later, outraged that my son and daughter aren't allowed to keep what is theirs, and yet still, somehow, on the wrong side, an agent of the forces of darkness.

'Where did you take it?'

'The women's refuge in Kentish Town, I read about it in the local paper. They had nothing there for the kids at all.'

I don't know what to say. The frightened, unhappy children of frightened, unhappy women have nothing; we have two of everything. We give away some, a tiny fraction, of what we have too much of. What is there for me to be angry about?

'Why does it have to be us who gives them something? Why can't the Government?' asks Tom.

'The Government can't pay for everything,' says David. 'We've got to pay for some things ourselves.'

'We did,' says Tom. 'We paid for that computer ourselves.'

'I mean,' says David, 'that if we're worried about what's happening to poor people, we can't wait for the Government to do anything. We have to do what we think is right.'

'Well, I don't think this is right,' says Tom.

'Why not?'

'Because it's my computer.'

David merely flashes him a beatific smile.

'Why isn't it just their bad luck?' Molly asks him, and I laugh. 'Just your bad luck' was, until relatively recently, David's explanation for why our kids didn't own a Dreamcast, or a new Arsenal away shirt, or anything else that every other person at school owns.

'These children don't have much luck anyway,' David explains with the slow, over-confident patience of a recently created angel. 'Their dads have been hitting their mums, and they've had to run away from home and hide, and they haven't got their toys with them … You have lots of luck. Don't you want to help them?'

'A bit,' says Tom grudgingly. 'But not as much as a whole computer.'

'Let's go and see them,' says David. 'Then you can tell them that. You can say you want to help them a bit and then ask for your computer back.'

'David, this is outrageous.'

'Why?'

'You can't blackmail your own children like that.'

I'm beginning to feel better. I was struggling for a while back there, pinned back by the moral force of David's arguments, but now I can see that he's gone mad, that he wants to humiliate us all. How could I have forgotten that this is what always happens with zealots? They go too far, they lose all sense of appropriateness and logic, and ultimately they are interested in nobody but themselves, nothing but their own piousness.

David drums his fingers on the table and thinks furiously.

'No, I'm sorry, you're right. It is outrageous. I've overstepped the mark. Please forgive me.'

Shit.

796 words

© Nick Hornby, 2001

Annotations
Detritus (line 5): a loose mass or pile of material.
Kentish Town (line 31): a part of Greater London.

Worksheet: *How to be Good*

Comprehension

1. Locate the passage in Nick Hornby's *How to be Good* and summarise the story up to this point.
2. Describe the children's reaction to the fact that one of the computers has been given away and what this reaction tells the reader.
3. Identify the point of view the author uses in this scene and comment on its importance for the reader.

Analysis

Choose *one* of the following tasks. Write 200–300 words.

1. Characterise David as he is presented to us in this scene. Is the David we meet here typical of the character throughout the novel?
2. How does Katie cope with the conflict in this scene?

Composition

Choose *one* of the following tasks.
Write a minimum of 200–300 words.

1. Nick Hornby is one of Britain's most popular contemporary writers. Write a review of *How to be Good* for an English magazine.
2. *GoodNews* describes the "possessions game" as something that makes people "lazy and spoiled and uncaring." (p. 127).
   Write a comment on this opinion. You should refer to examples from the book itself as well as from other sources.

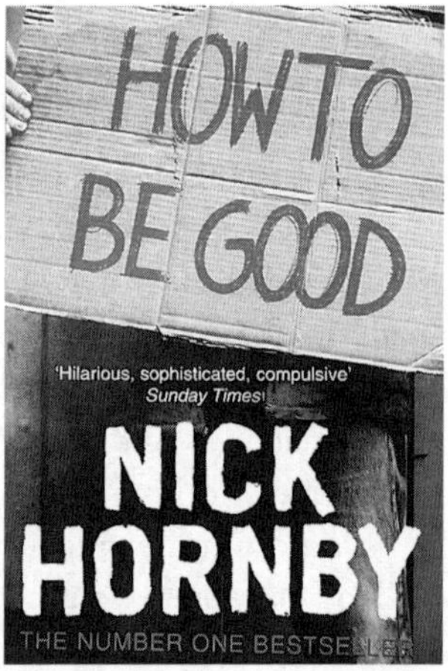

© *Liam Cleary*

Key: *How to be Good*

Comprehension

1. *Locate the passage in Nick Hornby's* How to be Good *and summarise the story up to this point.*

When asked to summarise a text or story it is important to keep the following points in mind:

- Use **your own words**.
- Concentrate on **the main facts** of the story up to this point.
- Get as much information into your summary as possible.
- For this question it is important to include **DJ GoodNews** in the summary and to refer to his effect on David.
- You might also make mention of **the conflict** that the change in David brings about.

David and Katie Carr, a middle-aged, middle-class couple, live in Holloway, London with their children Tom and Molly. The story begins in Leeds from where Katie tells David by phone that she does not want to be married to him any longer. Katie, a GP who entered her profession to do good deeds, is having an affair with Stephen. David, a columnist and 'the angriest man in Holloway', is a bitter, frustrated husband. Nick Hornby describes the battle the couple are waging with one another. Katie tells her brother and Becca, another GP, of the situation she finds herself in but continues to meet Stephen. She is, however, more guilt-ridden and worried than happy. The story takes a new twist when David goes to 'faith healer cum quack doctor' DJ GoodNews for treatment for his back. He annoys Katie by praising him and by now the children have gathered that all is not well. Tensions begin to rise in the house. David announces he is going away for a couple of nights. Katie meets Stephen again only to return to find David back again and a changed man. He wants them to try and rebuild their lives, becomes unbearingly goody-goody, gives money to complete strangers, ignores calls from his editor and has become a happy person. At first Katie thinks like a doctor in an effort to explain the change in her husband but it turns out he has come under the influence of DJ GoodNews, **thus setting in motion a** conflict that is at the heart of the rest of the story. **The passage cited here** occurs approximately one third of the way into the novel shortly after David and Katie have had a long discussion about DJ GoodNews.

2. *Describe the children's reaction to the fact that one of the computers has been given away and what this reaction tells the reader.*

   The children are clearly angry and upset. Alone their physical behaviour tells the reader this much as Tom is "shouting" and Molly "crying" when Katie walks in the door. Tom in particular is incensed as it is his computer that has been given away and his eyes we are told are "glistening, either with fury or tears". In addition Tom, unlike Molly, doesn't cry very often so his anger is obvious. Both children then question the correctness of the decision to give away the computer. Tom wants to know why the government can't be the one to do such benevolent deeds and reminds his father that he paid for his computer with his own money. Molly, too, questions her father's decision though one senses that her grief is slightly milder than that of her brother. After all, she still has her own computer even if she will have to share it from now on. Tom sums up the children's reaction and attitude to their father's action in one blunt sentence when he says "I don't think this is right". Eventually, with their mother's support, they get their father to admit as much. Their reaction shows the reader they are two very normal children, both intelligent and able to defend themselves. More importantly, their reaction around which the scene is built draws attention to the split between the parents and the extent to which David has been converted to good deeds. Katie's plight, and her ignorance of the man she calls her husband, is very clear here.

3. *Identify the point of view the author uses in this scene and comment on its importance for the reader?*

   In this scene author Nick Hornby presents the actions and happenings through the eyes of Katie Carr in the first person. This begins with "I come home the next night to the sound of trouble …" and continues in the first person as everything is described as Katie sees it. "David and the kids are sitting …" It is not only what Katie sees that is told in the first person but also what she feels. "I'm beginning to feel better. I was struggling for a while back there …" This choice of first person narrative is very important for the reader's assessment of the novel. The reader is faced with the task of judging for him or herself how much one can trust what Katie is telling us. A vital part of assessing this novel, its rights and wrongs, its strengths and weaknesses, is based on coming to a conclusion on this matter. How reliable is the information Katie gives us? Is she biased or objective? This in turn helps us get to know the character of Katie better and is one reason the author probably chose this point of view. He does not want us to be neutral towards her but wants us to feel and understand the situation she finds herself in.

Analysis

1. *Characterise David as he is presented to us in this scene. Is the David we meet here typical of the character throughout the novel?*

For this question the general rules for characterisation still apply. It is important to remember to

- study **his behaviour** carefully.
- analyse everything he says and consider **what others say about him**.
- examine **his children's attitude to him** and their reaction to his decision to sell the computer.
- ask yourself **how Katie reacts** to the situation she walks in on and what that tells us about her.
- try and contrast this David with the David we meet at the start and at other parts of the story.

At one level David Carr comes across in this scene as a person who is kind, soft-spoken, sincere, patient, apologetic. He is a man with a social conscience and wants to help the needy. Therefore he has given away a computer to a women's refuge home. When he meets protest from his children because of this he apologises for "overstepping the mark". However, one can read far more into this character and his actions. Some people might ask the question "Is this guy for real?" Certainly his wife has started doing that. After all David has not given his own computer away but that of his son. Many would see this as a selfish and cruel thing to do. It is all the more cruel because he never consulted his son about this. He defends his action by saying the children don't need two computers as they are never on the computer at the same time. Throughout the whole scene he conducts himself as if he were talking to adults, as if what he has done is something straightforward and in no way outrageous or difficult to understand. He makes his children feel guilty about the matter by reminding them how little some children have and by suggesting they go and ask for the computer back. This all amounts to a type of moral blackmail, the actions of a hypocrite. His children's reactions however show the reader how much of a patronizing bully and 'zealot' this man is. As a character he is very difficult to deal with for the three other members of his family. When he is chastised he immediately apologises and there is very little they can do about the matter. **All this is in sharp contrast** to, and untypical of, the David the reader knows from the start of the book; the angriest man in Holloway, aggressive, impolite and hard to live with. He is a man who earns his living by complaining about things in a newspaper column. Katie, for her part, doesn't "know what to say". She sees the change in her husband as a sort of religious conversion for which there is no logical explanation. Later on in the book David mellows somewhat and becomes less irritating. He is no longer the goody goody David Carr who is driving his wife and children slowly round the bend but a man who she discovers she can live with even if there is much about him which she knows she will never change.

2. *How does Katie cope with the conflict in this scene?*

When answering this question it is important to concentrate on
- what Katie says in the course of the scene.
- anything else that would cast light on her reaction to the fight e. g. behaviour, thoughts, etc.

In many ways Katie is the only possible referee in this family squabble which she walks in on. Nevertheless, it is interesting to note that the way she copes with the conflict is not to act as a referee but to eventually enter into it and take a definite stance of her own on the issue. This stance, in keeping with her ongoing marital difficulties, is to take the side of the children against her husband David. The author shows us how Katie copes with this conflict not only by telling us what she says but also what she thinks. Her initial move is to question David as to why he has done this without consulting anyone. She then recalls that it was David who wanted to buy two computers despite her protests to the contrary. This makes her feel "outraged" and very much on the side of her children in the conflict. She still manages to keep her cool and questions her husband further. His answer to this sets her back for she knows that theoretically he is right when he says that the women in the refuge home have nothing at all. Her silence as the quarrel continues shows her ability to listen but finally she comes down on the side of the children and accuses her husband of outrageous behaviour and of blackmailing the children. **All in all**, she copes with the conflict well by not becoming too embroiled in it while at the same time making clear to her husband, who she suspects may be going mad, that what he has done is just not acceptable.

Composition

1. *Nick Hornby is one of Britain's most popular contemporary writers. Write a review of* How to be Good *for an English magazine.*

When writing a review of a book attention should be paid to the following points:

- What can the readers expect if they read the book in question? Does the book belong to **a certain genre**? Is it a **mystery**, **adventure**, **or romance**?
- What do you like or dislike about the book's writing style?
- Does it give you **a sense of the place or period** in which it's set? What is the **author's/narrator's** "**voice**" like?
- Mention **the name of the author and the book title in the first paragraph** and get the theme of the book across in the beginning of your review.
- Try using **a few short quotes** from the book to illustrate your points. Give the reader a sense of the author's writing style.
- A good review expresses **the reviewer's opinion** and persuades the reader to read the book or to avoid reading it altogether.
- A review tells the reader a lot about the book but **not too much**. In the case of *How to be Good* make sure you **do not reveal** how the marital struggle ends.
- Do some research about the author, in this case Nick Hornby. Biographical information gives your review a sense of depth.

Having not read any of Nick Hornby's previous works – *Fever Pitch, High Fidelity* or *About a Boy* – it was hard to know what to expect from *How to be Good.* Friends who'd bought it raved about it:
"You must read it ... you have to ... you mean you haven't???" All I knew was that he's an incredibly funny, witty, clever, bestselling writer whose books have all been made into films. Hmmm. Well now I have read How to be Good and I am a great deal wiser.
The opening sentence "I am in a car park in Leeds when I tell my husband I don't want to be married to him any more" sets the stage and establishes the main theme of a woman struggling to come to terms with her failing marriage. Katie Carr, a middle-aged, middle class GP, is married to columnist David, the "angriest man in Holloway" but she has started an affair with Stephen, the one thing no good wife or mother does. And being good is

what this story is about. Katie has always been good, a good doctor doing good things for people, a good mother, a good wife. In fact being good is at the heart of all her worries. Or rather not being good for Hornby cleverly places Katie in a highly uncomfortable position by turning David, her grouchy husband of many years, into a born-again father, husband and social do-gooder after David visits DJ GoodNews, his new friend, soul mate, guru and comrade in arms against all forms of social injustice. To Katie's understandable horror GoodNews eventually moves in with the family at 32 Webster Road. And so the reader follows the Carr family on the rocky road to nowhere.

And it is on this rocky road that the book comes to grief. **After a bright start** Hornby's story peters out into a very average, run-of-the-mill tale of married life in modern England. I personally found myself wishing Katie Carr would just walk out on him or disappear altogether. "In a way, I wish I did have a headache, but I don't; I just have a soul-ache, and I want it taken away, whatever the cost. I have given up. I have not been able to beat them so I will join them." The initial sympathy the reader feels towards Katie doesn't take long to wear thin. The desire to skip a page or two increases with every extra piece of semi-confessional narrative.

This is not to say there isn't much that is – dare I say it – *good* about this book. I even laughed once or twice. Hornby is particularly strong when it comes to portraying the nitty-gritty details of a family in distress, of life in Eastender, New Labour London, though at times he overtaxes even his most loyal fans as, for example, when he presents us with an entire page consisting only of a list of the names of people David Carr dislikes. Despite its strong dialogue and convincing tone How to be Good remains an iffy, banal, uninspiring story. No doubt it too will sell well and be made into a successful film.

2. GoodNews *describes the "possessions game" as something that makes people "lazy and spoiled and uncaring (p. 127). Write a comment on this opinion. You should refer to examples from the book itself as well as from other sources.*

The aspects of writing a comment which you should keep in mind are:

- You are being asked for your opinions here and must give them if the answer is to be complete. That does not mean you have to fully agree or disagree with the topic but **you must say what you think**.
- **Knowledge of the general topic** which can be incorporated into your answer **is vital**. These might include facts, statistics, quotes and so on.
- First of all, state the problem or issue at hand and then give your opinion on it.
- Find **reasons for your opinion**. This is the evidence to support your claim.
- In this particular question think of good examples from How to be Good to support what you believe to be true.
- Concentrate on **language and content**.

The issue raised by GoodNews when he makes this statement is one that should be **of the utmost importance** to us all. Behind the "possessions game", as he calls it, are other fundamental questions such as why some countries are stupendously rich and others horrendously poor, how this imbalance can be changed and how people can be got to think about other values in life such as helping others. As with a number of the arguments made by GoodNews and David throughout the book they have right on their side. Some African countries have per capita income levels of around $1 a day, figures in stark contrast to the earnings of a man like David Beckham. Many experts have frequently pointed out that help from rich nations would go a long way to relieving the problems of poor countries. Not only that but increased donations from those wealthy sections of the population in England would help tremendously towards alleviating the plight of the poor, the ill or the homeless in England. Hence GoodNews' explanation as to why he does not want a dishwasher: "When the last peasant in the Brazilian rainforest has a dishwasher.. then count me in, yeah? But until then I'm making a stand."

As one might expect, he is written off as mad by Katie. **The reality of the matter is** that acquiring possessions can make people lazy, spoiled and uncaring. Such people become exceedingly selfish and caught up in a world that is so rich it does not realise how well off it is. There is no better proof of this than Katie's daughter Molly who announces to her mother's horror that "everybody in the world's got a dishwasher." Molly, a selfish and not particularly likeable individual, has grown up knowing only people who own dishwashers, DVDs and so on. Children such as Molly and Tom are products of the possessions game and Katie realises this. The significance of the fact that Molly and Tom are made help with the wash-up is not lost on the reader of How to be Good. In today's world, as we experience it, people have lost a sense of what should be important, of what should matter. This is not to say that GoodNews and people like him are the solution to the problem. After all, GoodNews is partly a sponger, David a pious convert to a cause he only partially understands. That they do good deeds is beyond doubt but there is little to be gained if people preach to others all the time – what is needed most of all to solve the poverty in the poorer sections of our world are funds and further urgent action such as Live Aid as well as improved general education to make people concentrate on focusing on the needy and not on the possessions game.

Celebrating conformity: Disney's Mickey Mouse utopia

In this exclusive online essay Jenny Diski examines two accounts of life in Disney's new town, Celebration, USA.

Jenny Diski
Tuesday August 15, 2000
The Guardian

For a committed sedentary like myself, one of the most striking aspects of the populating of the town of Celebration, Florida, built by the Disney Corporation in the late 1990s, was the ease with which people made the decision to sell up and move there. In some cases, they crossed the continent, gave up substantial careers, took the kids out of school, put their property on the market, and signed a financial commitment to buy a plot of land on which not a single brick had been laid, in an alligator-infested swamp owned by a corporation which specialised in producing cartoons and simulations of historical and geographical clichés. Some people just popped in after a trip to next-door Disneyland and signed up for a new existence, others packed up and moved to rented accommodation nearby in order to be on the spot when the lottery for the first plots of land was announced.

You don't have to drive for very long in the States before you find yourself stuck behind a slow-moving house. Not one of those recreational vehicles that might as well be a house, but an honest to goodness two-bedroom, living-room, kitchen and bathroom house that will, when it arrives where it is going, be fixed on elevated bricks and be called home by its inhabitants. At least for a while. The buildings in America may be on the move, but it's nothing compared to the lack of fixity of the people. Even houses that are built in situ, in towns and suburbs, have, no matter what the diversity of architectural style, an air of slightly rackety impermanence, as if their original builders had settled only for as long as it took for word to arrive of somewhere better. People in America move. They always have. They moved to get there in the first place, and then moved again for land, gold, work or just the thrill of going somewhere new. Ghost towns stand as relics of this tradition, signposted with pride as if their empty, decayed structures told the American story better than the towns and cities presently throbbing with living inhabitants who for the most part have come from somewhere else, or are going there. To be in one spot is a kind of limbo, whereas the ghost town's echo of an extinct past, of people upped and gone, the sense of a place utilised and then forsaken seems to speak of the romantic vigour of those who moved on, more than the waste and abandonment of what they left behind. The itinerant town was an essential component of the making of America. As the tracks were being laid across the wilderness by the railroad companies in their frantic race to bridge the Atlantic and Pacific coasts, supply trains brought the workers and their materials, along with the entire makings of an instant town for the labourers to sleep, eat and play in. These were the original hell on wheels, entire prefabricated buildings, broken down into their clapboard parts like flats for a stage set, and, travelling in the coaches behind, the saloon keepers, prostitutes, restaurateurs, gamblers and other essential personnel ready to set up the whole town in a day at the current furthest extent of the railroad. Whereupon life, death, drinking, whoring, gambling, fighting and doubtless a little quiet poetic contemplation went on until the railroad tracks had been laid beyond a certain outer limit, when the whole kit and caboodle was taken down, put back on the train and trundled off to the next stopping place.

There is no special mention of this restless tendency in either of these books[1] on the town of Celebration, but for a European, the rootlessness of Americans is a central curiosity, and in this case a factor the several authors fail to take into account in judging the degree to which families and individuals were really committing themselves in buying into the Disney dream life. The power of Disney in the psyche of America accounts for a good deal of their blind trust, but the readiness of people of all ages and classes to disrupt their lives and move elsewhere underlies and possibly undercuts that trust. Belief that Disney could turn its own fantasy into their reality persuaded people to take large risks.

'People trusted Disney,' said one resident. 'They trusted that Disney standards would ensure that the community they were going to live in would be better than most, if not superbly better than most. I think that is the only reason most people came here.' The original planners of Celebration themselves feared the Disneyphiles they would attract, the ones 'who go to Disney World eight times a year and think that because Main Street is clean they can extrapolate that to a community. Those are the people who think their kids will never get a B in school and there is never going to be a weed in their lawn when they move to Celebration.'

None of this prevented the Corporation from blazoning the literature with Disney's name and putting a 30 per cent premium on local property prices for

1 The Celebration Chronicles: Life, Liberty and the Pursuit of Property Value in Disney's New Town by Andrew Ross. Verso, 340 pp., £17, Celebration, USA: Living in Disney's Brave New Town by Douglas Frantz and Catherine Collins. Holt, 342 pp., £18.99, 23 September 1999

unbuilt houses as an entrance fee to the Disney town. But the risks and the naivety of those who paid their dollars to Disney were diluted by their sheer willingness to move and then move on. If the pixie dust turned to dandruff you could always call U-Haul and wash it out of your hair. Ken and Patti and their three teenage children had already relocated from Minneapolis to San Antonio. 'It was two days before the lottery at Celebration, so I flew down and entered it. We didn't really know much about Celebration, but we decided to try it anyway. We figured if it didn't work out, we could always move again.'

This article first appeared in the LONDON REVIEW OF BOOKS; Vol. 22 No. 16. www.lrb.co.uk *(1111 words)*

Annotations
in situ (line 19): in the natural position
caboodle (line 44): lot

Worksheet: Celebrating conformity

Comprehension

1. Describe the sacrifices people were prepared to make in order to live in the town of Celebration?
2. What reasons do you think explain why people were prepared to move to Celebration?
3. Identify the most obvious characteristic of American housing and the importance the author of this review attaches to it.

Analysis

Choose *one* of the following tasks. Write 200–300 words.

1. Assess the role of towns in American history as reflected in the text.
2. Contrast the attitudes of the men who planned Celebration with those of the people who actually came to live in the town.

Composition

Choose *one* of the following tasks. Write a minimum of 200–300 words.

1. "Home is where the heart is."
   Write an essay on the above quotation in the light of the text you have just read and other ideas you may have on the matter.
2. Write an essay in which you define the "American Dream" and discuss its influence on people of yesterday and today?

Key: Celebrating conformity

Comprehension

1. *Describe the sacrifices people were prepared to make in order to live in the town of Celebration?*

   The people who moved to the town of Celebration made many different sacrifices in order to do so. Generally-speaking, they gave up the security and steadiness of a settled life in order to buy into the Walt Disney dream of a fantastic new life that Celebration seemed to offer them. This meant that they had to sell up and leave the place they were living in. It also meant they had to disrupt family life and take their children out of school. In addition to this they gave up what, in many cases, were successful careers and good jobs in order to buy a piece of land in a swampy area on which they would one day build a house. For many of the people involved in this scheme that also entailed a long, long journey across the American continent or a flight down to Florida. Basically, they had to give up everything they had known and owned up until now, uproot the entire family, and head off to another part of America in order to have a chance of living in Celebration.

2. *What reasons do you think explain why people were prepared to move to Celebration?*

   When answering the question you should
   - look for reasons within the text itself.
   - try and come up with reasons of your own. The question is not limited to information in the text.

There are undoubtedly many varying factors which account for this but the first and foremost reason is the attraction and magnetism of the Disney name. People were prepared to take a chance and give up all they had in order to be associated with a Disney scheme. The name of Disney has over the years become an American symbol for success and the realisation of dreams. Disney World and Disneyland belong to every American's childhood and are associated with a happy ending, a world in which nothing goes wrong. Hence, those people who were buying into the town of Celebration fully believed nothing would go wrong because it was a Disney town. The author of this review also points to the rootlessness of American people as a significant factor in this whole process. She points to many different aspects of the American character and American life which go to explain the ease with which many people just left for Celebration. Ghost towns are one of the things she refers to in this context. **The bottom line** as far as she is concerned is that Americans are always on the move. I, however, believe that **other factors should not be forgotten** here although the author does not mention them. One of these would be people's dissatisfaction with their own lives. I expect that many of those who moved to Celebration were, deep down, unhappy with the lives they were leading. This would have made it easier, and more attractive, to take a chance on Celebration. In addition, the belief many Americans have in the American dream means that they are perhaps more ready to have a go at achieving their dreams than Europeans would be. All these factors lay behind such readiness to move to Celebration.

3. *Identify the most obvious characteristic of American housing and the importance the author of this review attaches to it.*

As far as the author is concerned American housing is not fixed and settled in one place but impermanent and forever on the move. The author refers to the houses one sees being pulled by car on American roads. These houses will stop somewhere and stay in that place until the owners feel it is time to move on. Housing in suburbs has that look also – as if the people in them are just waiting for the next move. This is important because it helps tell the American story and explains why people were able to move so easily to the town of Celebration in the 1990s. This is further seen in the likes of ghost towns where the deserted houses tell of a past history where people came, looked around and moved on. They are still doing it today and if Celebration is anything to go by they will continue to do it in the future.

Analysis

1. *Assess the role of towns in American history as reflected in the text.*

This question demands you
- read the text from start to finish for evidence to use in your answer.
- use your own descriptions and come to a conclusion as to **the function of towns in American history**.
- remember that to assess something is to **evaluate it** and it is not enough to describe it.

The text outlines the types of towns Americans have built in the course of their short history. Many of these were itinerant, instantly-founded places. The author refers to the fact that the process of building America involved the building of such towns and then deserting them. These ghost towns are preserved today and have attained a symbolic significance for all Americans. People such as gold diggers arrived in a place, took their chance and moved on. This was a development that lay at the heart of the American dream. Many towns today retain this lack of permanence. From the text we gather that a town does not mean the same thing to a European and an American. Although the text does not explicitly say so, European attitudes tend to see a town as a place to converge on and perhaps settle down in. Americans have always placed a different value on towns. Towns are seen as part of their journey, places that serve a purpose for a while and that will one day be left behind. All in all, the author of this text sees towns in America as central to the growth of modern America. They are places that sprang up out of a definite, temporary need and in those cases where the need no longer existed they simply died out. They are also important in that they bear testimony to the rootlessness and restlessness of Americans.

2. *Contrast the attitudes of the men who planned Celebration with those of the people who actually came to live in the town.*

Keep in mind that in order to contrast these two matters you must
- hone in on **the differences** between them.
- search the text for the solution. This is not a general question but one specifically related to the text.
- **underline the differences** as you meet them and then describe them in your own words.

Nothing could be as different as the attitudes of the planners to the project and the attitudes of the people who ended up living in the town of Celebration. From the very start the planners were worried about the type of people Celebration would attract. They feared they would be fans of Disney who believed everything would be perfect there. To a certain extent they were right because it was this faith in Disney, and the world Disney would build for them in Celebration, that made many people decide to buy a plot and house there. These people were trusting and gullible. Indeed some would say they were stupid and blind in their whole approach to the project. This is not something one can say about the planners. They were ruthless and profit driven even though they had doubts about many aspects of the job in hand. They placed extra premiums on property and charged a fee for actually entering the town. As well as that they used every opportunity to advertise the Disney name. Whereas the people who came to live in Celebration were carefree and took a chance, the town planners were calculating and somewhat cruel in their approach.

Composition

1. *"Home is where the heart is."*
   Write an essay on the above quotation in the light of the text you have just read and other ideas you may have on the matter.

Be careful to do the following when answering this question:

- Before you begin, gather together, either mentally or in note form, the **main ideas** of your essay.
- Have a definite idea before you start on how you intend to argue the point and how you intend to conclude.
- Try and come up with a **useful quotation** or two around which you can build your arguments.
- Check your spelling and punctuation.
- Work out exactly what the concept home can mean and what role it plays in the text you have read.

Home is a concept most people grow up with. There are exceptions to this rule but in most cases each and every one of us knows what home means. **For the vast majority of people** home is the house and place one spends one's childhood in. That may be a village outside of Bombay, a town in Nebraska or an island off the coast of Queensland. We think of our parents, relations and friends when we think of home. We call to mind the smells and sights we associate with that place. Home is a theme we speak about quite often and about which we have definite feelings, ideas and opinions. Yet the whole issue of home is a difficult one to make general statements about. Is home the same thing for all people or is it more a case that, as the title of this essay suggests, home is where you are happiest?

Consider for a moment the Americans who live in houses which they regularly move from place to place. Or those who went to live in Celebration, Florida. Where is home to them? Think about the person who decides to leave, or is forced to leave, the town, homeland or country in which he grows up. "I pity the poor immigrant who wishes he would have stayed home" sang Bob Dylan on his John Wesley Harding album. After such an immigrant has spent much of his or her life in two different parts of the world where is he at home? If as Dylan says "... he wishes he would have stayed home ..." then the question is easily answered – home is the Heimat, the place he left and wishes he had not left. But what if he has made a success of his life and is a wealthy, healthy, well-thought of person in the USA, Britain or Australia. Where is home for him? Is it not a case that he is just as much at home in the New World as he could be in the Old?

And then there is the issue of the person who is at home when in the company of a certain person or people rather than in a place. Many people leave home because they get married. This can entail a move to the next town, county or country. It can also take a person across the world. Is such a person not at home where the heart is happy?

Personally-speaking I come down on the side of the title of this essay. Home – in the general sense – is where the heart is, where one feels happiest, where one belongs. The place we are born in and grow up in is a different matter. Deep inside us definite memories and feelings will always cling to that place and they cannot be found anywhere else in the world.

2. *Write an essay in which you define the "American Dream" and discuss its influence on people of yesterday and today?*

If you take on this question unless you should be able to

- **define** properly what is meant by **the American Dream**.
- assemble a number of ideas on the issue and support them with historical, political or sociological references.

Men and women have always wanted material wealth and professional success. It is a powerful human desire, one that held true when Judas betrayed Jesus and still holds true today. People will go to great lengths in their pursuit of personal ambitions, wealth or fame. As many people have learned to their cost, however, wanting something and getting it are not one and the same. The popular term used to describe this idea of personal or professional gain in an American context is the American Dream. The notion of the 'American Dream' started as a strong motivation not only for Americans, trying to build their lives through hard work and sacrifice, but also for immigrants, coming to America for a chance at that elusive but inspiring 'dream.' As many historians have pointed out there have in fact been a number of American Dreams that have formed American identity from the time of the Pilgrims to the present day. There has been the Pilgrim American dream which was basically a search for religious freedom that brought the first immigrants to the "New World". There has also been the dream of political freedom promised in the Declaration as well as the dreams of upward mobility and of home ownership not to mention the more recent idealistic dream of equality as articulated by Martin Luther King, in his 'I Have a Dream' speech. Nowadays the version of the American Dream that dominates is one of personal fulfilment, of fame and fortune, of Disney World and Hollywood. The American Dream is as important in today's culture as it was three hundred years ago. We have state lotteries that promise instant millions. We have Las Vegas, Wall Street and Pretty Woman. We have quiz shows that guarantee instant fortunes and our young people have role models who have attained this fame and fortune in one form or another be it in the fields of sport, music or film. On the other hand we must acknowledge the poor and homeless in George Bush's America, the drug addicts, the alcoholic stars, the forgotten minorities. Tinsel town is one side of the story but as the saying goes "Everything that glitters is not gold". Unfortunately, the American Dream is, and has always been, a double edged sword. For all the Henry Fords and Ronald Reagans America has produced there have been many millions who never made it. And ghost towns are as much a part of US history as is downtown New York. Yet this American Dream remains part and parcel of modern America and one cannot understand Americans without first understanding their dreams.

Non-literary texts

So just why is the Daily Meldrew so grumpy?

Why is the Daily Mail so successful? It isn't only those of a leftish persuasion who are mystified by the Mail's circulation rise over the past decade. Even people who should know better, such as journalists, too often ascribe its triumph solely to its generous editorial budget. The money helps, of course, but that doesn't begin to explain why the Mail has managed to forge such a close bond with its readers, selling 2.4m. Since its 1971 reinvention as a "quality tabloid" under David English, and much more so since the editorship passed to Paul Dacre in 1992, the Mail has emerged as a sort of middle-class bible. But its message tends to be of the fundamentalist, Old Testament variety, all fire and brimstone, reinforcing and exacerbating the perceptions – and misconceptions – of its audience, fortifying their siege mentality and entrenching their prejudices.

Its continual accentuating of the negative, decrying change and preaching against the evolution of a liberal, multi-cultural society, echoes the concerns of a largely white population which, despite its relative affluence and the realisation of its social aspirations, remains deeply suspicious of modern Britain. No wonder a Mori poll identified a generation of grumpy, dissatisfied, middle-aged men as the Meldrews. Their material conditions have changed for the better – as Guardian columnist Polly Toynbee rightly pointed out – but this hasn't affected their perception that they are off to hell in a handcart. These people form the natural constituency of the paper that taps into, and then nourishes, their pessimism and scepticism, highlighting a whole range of reactionary attitudes.

A study of the past month's issues of the Daily Mail proves that its real title should be the Daily Meldrew. Playing to the fears and narrow-mindedness of its audience, it magnifies their xenophobia and hypochondria, panders to their envy and, despite its vaunted image as a paper sympathetic to women, disparages feminism. What follows is a random sample of headlines, stories and features that illustrate those points. I have specifically omitted coverage of the Soham murders, I haven't dealt with leader columns which are read by only a minority, and I have ignored Westminster politics. I must make clear that I'm not challenging the authenticity and factual accuracy of the Mail's stories (though, in some cases, I could). What is fascinating is their selection, placement, repetition and – in the case of features – the way they are heavily angled, often with headlines asking rhetorical questions.

Let's begin with the knocking of our country. An article headlined "Dickensian Britain" suggested life hasn't improved much in the past 150 years. Another, by a former magistrate (and, incidentally, ex-Sunday Telegraph editor), was supposed to "make your hair stand on end". A third, "How Britain is destroying itself", was followed by a piece which decries "the insidious and inexorable march of political correctness". Now to the specific peril we face, immigration, which over the 26 days of August I studied accounted for more spreads and page leads than any other topic. The month began with a page about non-white Britons having a higher birthrate, and here is a handful of headlines in subsequent days and weeks: "250,000 migrants a year entering Britain"; "Farce of asylum crackdown"; "Luxury centre for failed immigrants' last days in the UK"; "Asylum seekers will be bribed to go home"; "Asylum seekers will get £50,000 to pay for their driving lessons".

One story that ran and ran began with the revelation that a group helping people to fight deportation had been given a national lottery grant of £340,000: "Is this the barmiest lottery handout of them all?" (...) It was noticeable that the paper hailed for its women-friendly Femail pages maintains a traditional view of the female role. "Why women should learn to love doing housework" trilled one headline. Another suggested "how to practise the lost art of flirting". A column by Melanie Phillips about girls' greater success at passing exams than boys, claimed it was due to a "feminist lie that lets boys down". (I can't resist pointing out that girls were performing better at exams 40 years ago, long before teachers were influenced by feminism).

Women often appear in the Mail in bikinis, with features such as "Have they or haven't they?" (on breast implants). Most of the pictures were of celebrities. Now the Mail understands that people love reading about celebrities but it doesn't appear to like them, consistently presenting them in a poor light, doubtless believing that its readers are jealous of their fame and riches. Again, we should note the devious, and devastating, use of the query at the end of these headlines. It's a trademark of such features which allows the wildest of speculation to be presented as fact.

"He is the miner's son who married an aristocrat ... but did Bryan Ferry's marriage ultimately fail because he is too in love with himself?" ... "Less Hurley. As her curves shrink alarmingly, is Liz overdoing the diet regime?" ...

"What do women see in this man [Andre Previn]?" … "Who Dunaway with her [Faye's] money?" The Mail also asked one day if Jonathan Ross's marriage was doomed to failure and answered itself a day or so later by picturing the couple together. Sometimes, it doesn't need the question marks. "Cocaine, booze and the sexual rumours that won't die. The truth about the body Jamie Lee's so proud of". Britney Spears got a lot of attention: "Porn again Britney: alcohol, binge-eating and pornography – how the 'virginal' Miss Spears has been driven to the brink by stardom".

Knock, knock, knock. The Mail presents every facet of life in as gloomy and threatening a light as possible. There were pieces attacking the BBC, the NHS, the education system, GM foods and several questioning judicial sentencing policy. If there are so many Meldrews about in Britain, could it be entirely due to the Daily Meldrew? 976 words

© *The Guardian, Septmeber 2, 2002*

Annotations

Meldrew (line 1): Victor Meldrew, a British hero of the 1990s. He believes everybody is against him. Meldrew eventually became a term that referred to negative people between 35–60

Mori (line 17): a polling organisation

Soham murders (line 30): the murder of two girls in Cambridgeshire which horrified Britain in 2002.

barmiest (line 51): craziest

trilled (line 54): sang, warbled

Andre Previn (line 70): famous conductor and composer

Jonathan Ross (line 71): TV presenter

Jamie Lee (line 75): Jamie Lee Curtis

Worksheet: So just why is the Daily Meldrew so grumpy?

Comprehension

1. The Mail calls itself "a quality tabloid." Why do you think it does that and what is meant by the phrase?
2. What reasons does the author give for the newspaper's success?
3. Describe the typical Daily Mail reader. What kind of person is he or she?

Analysis

Choose *one* of the following tasks (write 200–300 words) or take the translation.

1. Analyse the Daily Mail's attitude to women as outlined in this article.
2. Contrast the British tabloid and broadsheet newspapers. You may refer to the article you have just read if you wish.

Translation

Translate the following text into good German or choose *one* of the analysis tasks.

The hate industry by Arun Kundnani,
Britain's tabloid media has become obsessed with 'scrounging' asylum seekers, out of control immigration, foreign 'plagues' and Muslim terrorists. The emerging politics of hate, fear and hysteria is set to dominate Britain in the near future. Following the anti-terrorist raids in Wood Green, north London, and the death of Detective Constable Stephen Oake during an anti-terrorist raid in Manchester, the nation's newspapers launched an unprecedented campaign against asylum seekers, encouraged by the supposed 'link' between terrorism and asylum. Suddenly, these two emotionally charged topics, hitherto kept mainly separate, have been fused into a morass of fear and insecurity. Newspaper articles throughout January solidified the link, leading most people in Britain to believe that the asylum system provides an 'open door' for terrorists to enter Britain. Clamping down on asylum seekers is thus no longer just about preventing 'abuse' by 'scroungers' but a matter of national security. Resentment has turned to fear and anger. And the media are cleverly manipulating this fear to legitimise ambitious changes to Britain's asylum, immigration and human rights policy. In fact, only a tiny handful of the hundreds of thousands of asylum seekers in Britain have been charged under the anti-terror laws.

© The Institute of Race Relations, London

Composition

Choose *one* of the following tasks. Write a minimum of 200–300 words.

1. Write an essay on the influence of the media on youth today
2. One night on Channel 4 you see a guest on a TV show play Russian Roulette and win! Write a dialogue between you and a friend which describes the feelings you experienced while watching this show and your angry opinions on the matter while your friend justifies the decision to allow such an act on television

Key: So just why is the Daily Meldrew so grumpy?

Comprehension

1. *The Mail calls itself "a quality tabloid." Why do you think it does that and what is meant by the phrase?*

- Here you are being asked to define something so make sure to give a **precise explanation** of what the phrase means.
- All definitions need to be exact if they are to be fully correct
- Also look for as many reasons as you can find as to why the mail calls itself that.

When the Daily Mail refers to itself as a "quality tabloid" it does so deliberately and for a reason. Tabloid newspapers are often referred to as the popular newspapers and sell in large numbers. Good examples of such newspapers would be the Sun, The Star or the Daily Mirror. The methods and journalism they use are, however, considered by many to be inferior to what one finds in quality broadsheet papers. They tend to be sensationalist and do not always place emphasis on the truth. Therefore, the Daily Mail calls itself a quality tabloid to show that although it has the form and style of a tabloid it also possess the quality of a broadsheet. It wants to be linked in people's minds to quality while having all the practical advantages of a tabloid. This places it at the top of the tabloid newspapers and establishes it as an alternative to the broadsheets.

2. *What reasons does the author give for the newspaper's success?*

Reasons for something are sometimes obvious but often hidden in the text. Therefore you have to

- read all the text, underlining or numbering reasons as you find them.
- sort them into important or less important ones.
- find a main reason and some others for the Mail's success.
- describe the reasons in your own words as much as possible.

The primary reason for the Mail's success is thought by many to be the generous amount of money at the Editor's disposal. This has allowed the editors to change the way the paper looks and increase sales. However, this author believes there is more to this than meets the eye. He goes on to give a number of other reasons which he believes explain the matter. He says that the paper was given a new upbeat, upmarket image in 1971 and then got a new editor in 1992. In the following years it became more and more conservative, traditionalist and extreme in its outlook. This appealed to a large section of the paper-reading British public and accounts in part for the success of the Mail. Yet the author also believes that **there is another factor one should not overlook** and that is the emphasis on all that is negative in British society. This too appeals to many well-off British citizens who see foreigners, thieves and liberals as the reason for life's woes. In other words, the Daily Mail plays on the worries of its readership in order to sell more papers and this is one of the prime reasons for its success.

3. *Describe the typical Daily Mail reader. What kind of person is he or she?*

The following should not be forgotten when attempting the answer:

- Describing a person or character demands you should first of all concentrate on any noteworthy features such as **age** or **social position**.
- In this case although it is a type of reader you are dealing with you the above rule still applies: **race, age, class, position, political views** or opinions and so on will all help answer the question.
- As you read through the text you should take note of when and how the author describes the typical Daily Mail reader. Then take these points and put them in a logical order.

The typical Daily Mail reader is a white, middle-aged British citizen who leans to the right in his or her political views and is probably quite comfortably off in financial terms. He may or may not be retired and enjoying life as a pensioner. As a person he or she is undoubtedly worried by what the person perceives as the threat to the British way of life, to British values and standards, which immigrants and other undesirables pose. **All in all**, he is a negative person, a person who has possibly not achieved all he wanted to in life. Life has been good to Daily Mail readers but they are not prepared to accept this and are more than ready to believe anything they read in their daily paper. He (or she) trusts only the people known to him and the type of life and ideas that have stood by him over the years.

Analysis

1. *Analyse the Daily Mail's attitude to women as outlined in this article.*

If asked to analyse an attitude (or opinion) be sure and

- thoroughly **examine the text from start to finish**.
- describe in detail what the question is looking for.
- concentrate on those passages that refer to the subject matter (in this case the newspaper's attitude to women).
- pay attention to such matters as **phrases, headlines, exclamation marks or question marks**.
- come to **a definite conclusion** as to the Mail's attitude. This should be expressed above all else by the use of adjectives you consider correct and suitable.

The Daily Mail's attitude to women is a very conservative and old-fashioned one. It tries to be friendly to women, like many of its male readers, but if women step out of line or do not do what the Mail thinks they should do then the Mail becomes very aggressive and bossy towards women. On the one hand women should, according to one headline "learn to love doing housework". Yet the Mail also presents women in bikinis, urges them to flirt and links feminism to boys' poor performance at exams. The women who suffer most of all at the hands of the Daily Mail are those women who have made it in one sphere or another in life, Examples would be actresses and singers. People such as Jamie Lee Curtis, Liz Hurley, Faye Dunaway and Britney Spears are attacked in the most devastating way and an image of them is created in the reader's mind which is more likely to be untrue than true. These are all women who do not conform to the Mail's idea of a "proper" woman, a woman who cooks and cares for her husband while at the same time being attractive, intelligent, well-qualified. The Mail's attitude to women is unfair, aggressive, and above all else warped.

2. *Contrast the British tabloid and broadsheet newspapers.*

It is important to remember that this particular question

- goes beyond the information in the text.
- requires you to already know a lot about **British newspapers**.
- does not limit itself to any one aspect of British newspapers so you must deal with **layout, style of reporting, themes** and so on.
- would be better answered if you can include a number of newspapers in the course of your answer and identify which type they are, tabloid or broadsheet.

There are many differences between tabloid and broadsheet newspapers. **The first distinction** is a physical one with the tabloids being half the page size of the broadsheets. In this sense the tabloid newspapers such as the Sun or the Mirror are not 'true' newspapers as they reject both the traditional form and content associated with broadsheets. Nevertheless the tabloids are text-based albeit with a heavy reliance on visual material. Tabloids tend to emphasise sensational news and to present it in a more simplfied, eye-catching form. Tabloids also use a great deal of informal language, slang and puns as well as big headlines **to catch readers' attention**. In addition they have few qualms about making use of invasive or offensive photographs to support their stories. They are often prepared to pay large sums of money to photographers – the infamous paparazzi, as they are known – for a particular photograph. The broadsheets **on the other hand** are known for their more objective reporting style, in particular their use of balanced and less inflammatory headlines, than the tabloid press. Quality broadsheets such as The Independent also cover a far wider spectrum of topics than the tabloids which tend to limit themselves to topical matters such as immigration and crime. The tabloids also run features across two pages more often, to make their page-as-unit the same or similar size to that of the broadsheet but, the amount of information included in the article tends to differ. A final difference worth mentioning is the use quality and tabloid newspapers make of headlines. A typical Daily Mail headline might be one such as is quoted here "Porn-again Britney: alcohol, binge-eating and pornography – how the virginal Miss Spears has been driven to the brink by stardom". This is in sharp contrast with the subheadings over Guardian articles e.g. "The Daily Mail is obsessed with knocking stories – but they help sell 2.4m copies." Sensational versus factual and that is perhaps the major difference between quality and tabloid newspapers.

Translation

Take note of the following if you decide to do the translation:

- Read the text a number of times.
- Avoid word for word translations. Your task is **to translate the meaning of the sentence**.
- If faced with a long and difficult sentence consider breaking it up into two shorter sentences.
- Try and retain the stress and speed in the sentence if at all possible.
- Watch out for "false friends", for adverbs, and **make sure you use the correct tense** when dealing with verbs.

Die britische Boulevardpresse ist von ‚schmarotzenden' Asylbewerbern, außer Kontrolle geratener Immigration, ausländischen ‚Seuchen' und muslimischen Terroristen besessen. Die neu entstehende Politik des Hasses, der Angst und der Hysterie wird Großbritannien in nächster Zukunft beherrschen. Nach den Antiterrorrazzien in Wood Green im Norden von London und nach dem Tod des Detective Constable Stephen Oake während einer Antiterrorrazzia in Manchester eröffneten die Zeitungen der Nation eine beispiellose Kampagne gegen Asylbewerber, ermutigt durch die angebliche ‚Verbindung' zwischen Terrorismus und Asyl. Plötzlich wurden diese beiden emotionsgeladenen, bisher zum großen Teil getrennt gehaltenen Themen in einem Morast der Furcht und der Unsicherheit vereinigt. Zeitungsberichte verfestigten den ganzen Januar hindurch diese Verbindung, was dazu führte, dass die meisten Leute in Großbritannien glauben, dass das Asylsystem den Terroristen ‚freien Eintritt' bietet. Wenn man bei Asylbewerbern strikter wird, geht es nicht mehr nur darum, ‚Missbrauch' durch ‚Schmarotzer' zu verhindern, sondern es geht um die nationale Sicherheit. Die Abneigung hat sich in Angst und Wut verwandelt. Und die Medien manipulieren geschickt diese Angst, um weitreichende Veränderungen in der britischen Asyl-, Einwanderungs- und Menschenrechtspolitik zu legitimieren. In Wirklichkeit wurde nur eine kleine Hand voll von den hunderttausend Asylbewerbern in Großbritannien nach den Antiterrorgesetzen angeklagt.

Composition

1. *Write an essay on the influence of the media on youth today.*

Make sure you keep the following in mind:

- Consider using a practical example from your own life or the life of a friend to open your essay.
- Find good examples of the influence exerted on youth.
- Try and incorporate some facts or figures into your essay.
- For such a topic as this one it is worth referring to both sides of the coin e. g. the good and the bad influence of the media.

My friend Alex seldom gets out. He's a TV junkie. I call round and he's watching this programme or that. When he's not in front of the box he's chatting on line or surfing. His father's big into digital radio so Alex knows about radio stations and places I've never heard of. **When I consider** Alex and many other of my friends there is little doubt in my mind but that the media exerts a huge influence on the youth of today. Media executives may be quick to deny this and to reject any responsibility for the part they play in youth violence, teenage pregnancies, smoking or alcoholism, not to mention bullying, but the facts speak for themselves. **Millions of dollars are spent each year in an effort to** get young people to buy this album, that brand of cigarettes, a certain type of car or cosmetics. Network executives and motion picture companies and others in the media will of course play down or even deny any impact their programs have on the attitudes and actions of youth. Nevertheless, **the truth of the matter is that**, each day, the average US teenager spends more time watching television than doing anything else – except sleeping. This amounts to over 20 hours a week on average with children from low-income or African-American backgrounds far exceeding this figure. Is it purely coincidence that rates of pregnancy, drug abuse and violence tend to be higher in these sociological groupings? Meanwhile, the TV networks, the press and other media forces continue to spend millions on special effects and marketing geared to increase appeal to youth markets. **The reality is that** there is money in youth spending and this is often exploited. Yet media influence on **the youth of today** is neither limited to these areas and nor is it totally negative. Many teenagers (32 % in one study in America) report that they learn about important health issues such as contraception from the newspapers, radio and television. Likewise with the advent of internet and the World Wide Web they have access to areas and information that their parents could never have dreamt of. This of course is not always a good thing. According to one conference paper produced in Stockholm there are over 200 racist websites operating out of Germany. Likewise the dangers of online chatting are well known. But young people can learn about countries, people, places and subjects which would otherwise be beyond their grasp. We can undoubtedly prove that the influence of media on the youth of today is huge and that it can be both of a negative and positive nature. What many people now tend to forget is that it is constantly changing. With the growing availability of computers changes occur much faster now and that proves the influence of the media. Unfortunately, this can have its downside too. Information on the web is often superficial, badly-presented or downright incorrect. Teaching the youth of today about this is a fundamental task if the influence of the modern media is to remain primarily a good thing.

2. *One night on Channel 4 you see a guest on a TV show play Russian Roulette and win! Write a dialogue between you and a friend which describes the feelings you experienced while watching this show and your angry opinions on the matter while your friend justifies the decision to allow such an act on television*

In order to write a good dialogue you need to
- keep language and content in mind.
- make sure you use **everyday, natural turns of phrase** (underlined below).
- use questions and exclamation marks.
- get an argument going – there are two opinions on this.
- justify the TV programme by introducing supporting arguments.
- also show the bad effects such a programme can have.
- add in **a bit of humour**.

ME: Hi Dave, how are you?
DAVE: Not too bad thank you. Any news mate?
ME: Not really. I'm just back from Anfield. Saw a cracker of a match against Leeds.
DAVE: Great wasn't it? Super finish from Owen!
ME: Yeah. Hey, come here, did you see the guy on Channel 4 last night. Mad wasn't it?

Dave: To be honest with you I haven't enjoyed a bit of TV as much in ages. I thought it was brilliant.

Me: You cannot be serious. Russian roulette! Live on TV! I agree it was heart stopping stuff but you cannot justify it. No way. Think of all the kids watching that programme. Don't be surprised if there are a few copycat performances over the next while. I don't know how anyone could allow that to happen. What kind of irresponsible fool allows such an act to go out live on television? He should get the sack instantly.

Dave: Ah come on, it was only a bit of fun. I reckon it was all set up and he knew what was going to happen.

Me: They say it wasn't an act and that he took a chance with his life. You can't justify that at any level.

Dave: Don't be so square. You have to admit it was exciting.

Me: I couldn't take my eyes off it – I'll give you that.

Dave: There, you see what I mean.

Me: Yes but it makes firearms look popular and nice. As if a gun couldn't hurt a fly. I'll bet you many people had nightmares after watching the show.

Dave: Perhaps, but I'll bet you nobody turned off their TV set. That's what the guys at Channel Four wanted, wasn't it?

Me: Undoubtedly, but you are forgetting one thing. Just because he does it on television does not make it right. In my opinion the use of a gun in that way in front of people should be a crime. I'm going home to write to the BBC. See ya.

Dave: Don't be such a drip mate. Can't you see the excitement in it, the thrill? If a guy is prepared to do such a thing who are you to say he shouldn't be allowed?

Me: For heaven's sake grow up Dave. You always were a bit of an idiot!

Dave: You watch what you are saying or I'll …

Me: Oooops, I'm off.

Whatever happened to protest?

Debate is presumably the essence of democracy. Yet today the feeling seems to be spreading that the imminence of war must suspend debate, that patriotic Americans must follow their leader, that challenging the presidential judgement is a form of lèse-majesté. When danger impends, the president must be accepted as the voice of a united nation. "What have we elected him for," observes one commentator, "if we are to act as if we expect our views to be treated as being of equal weight with his?"

This view raises a couple of questions that history might help us answer. The first is whether a democratic nation has a moral obligation to support the government when the republic is headed for war. The second is whether, as a factual matter, our ancestors have abstained from debate and dissent when their government was taking them toward war.

The answer to the first question is that going to war does not abrogate freedom of individual conscience and does not supersede the Bill of Rights. Even when the republic faces mortal dangers, the First Amendment to the Constitutions is still there. In the midst of the greatest war in American history, the Supreme Court in *West Virginia State Board of Education v. Barnette* held that a law compelling students in public schools to salute the flag and to recite the Pledge of Allegiance was unconstitutional. As Justice Robert H. Jackson said for the court, "If there is any fixed star in our constitutional constellation, it is that no official, higher or petty, can prescribe what shall be orthodox in politics, nationalism, religion, or other matters of opinion."

That decision was handed down on Flag Day, 1943. Though young Americans were fighting and dying for the American flag on many fronts around the planet, the court's stand against compulsory salutes and compulsory pledges of allegiance was generally applauded. Most Americans in 1943 thought the decision a pretty good statement of what we were fighting for.

The role of dissent is even more vital. Of all the decisions a free people must face, the question of war and peace is the most crucial. Before sending young Americans to kill and die in foreign lands, a democracy has a sacred obligation to permit full and searching discussion of the issues at stake. There is no obligation to bow down before an imperial presidency. The views of the American people should indeed have equal weight with those of the fellow they send to the White House.

As for the second question, the historical record shows that Americans have rarely refrained from criticism and dissent when the country was heading toward war. Even in the American Revolution, a third of the colonists, according to John Adams, opposed the drive toward independence. The War of 1812 provoked serious and strident dissent. The historian Samuel Eliot Morison called it "the most unpopular war that this country has ever waged, not even excepting the Vietnam conflict." President Madison's request for a declaration of war narrowly passed the Senate by 19 to 13 votes and the House of Representatives by 70 to 49. After war was declared, Gov. Caleb Strong of Massachusetts proclaimed a public fast to atone for a war "against the nation from which we are descended". Most New England governors turned down presidential requests for militia.

The Mexican War was almost as unpopular. There was fierce opposition to the declaration of war. In 1848 the House of Representatives itself resolved that the Mexican War had been "unnecessarily and unconstitutionally begun by the President of the United States." A few days later a young congressman attacked the presidential justification for the war as "from beginning to end, the sheerest deception." Explaining to a friend his opposition to the war, Rep. Abraham Lincoln of Illinois challenged what is known today as the Bush Doctrine of anticipatory self-defense: "Allow the President to invade a neighboring nation, whenever *he* shall deem it necessary to repel an invasion ... and you allow him to make war at pleasure." The Founding Fathers, he continued, "resolved to so frame the Constitution that *no one man* should hold the power of bringing this oppression upon us." Thirteen years later Abraham Lincoln, now president, faced a war of his own. The Civil War saw acute divisions even in the North. Men like Fernando Wood, former mayor of New York City and member of the House of Representatives, denounced Lincoln as a dictator and called for a negotiated peace.

The Spanish-American War, and especially the follow-up campaign against the Filipino insurrection, provoked vigorous criticism of the White House. "There are worse things than financial troubles in a Nation's career," wrote the great philosopher William James, explaining why he was supporting William Jennings Bryan against William McKinley in 1990. "To puke up its ancient soul, and the only things that gave it eminence among other nations, in five minutes and without a wink of squeamishness, is worse; and that is what Republicans would commit us to in the Philippines. Our conduct there has been one protracted infamy towards the Islanders, and one protracted lie towards ourselves." According to Mark Twain, the American flag should have "the white stripes painted black and the stars replaced by the skull and crossbones." What would Attorney General Ashcroft have done with so subversive a fellow Missourian?

The first world war was preceded by vigorous national discussion, and the debate before the second world war was the most angry and vicious of my lifetime – more savage than the debate over communism in the 1940s, or than the debate over McCarthyism in the 1950s, or than the debate over Vietnam in the 1960s. And most Americans today agree that the dissenters were right over Vietnam.

This is the historical record, and a proud record of debate and dissent it is. No administration has a right to send young Americans to kill and die in serious wars without the most frank and uninhibited national discussion. Let us not restore the imperial presidency. 1003 words

© *Newsweek Jan/Feb Special 2003*

Annotations
lèse-majesté (line 4): treason
abrogate (line 13): to officially cancel, to repeal or annul
to atone for (line 46): to make up for
squeamishness (line 69): easily sickened, frightened or shocked
infamy (line 71): the state of being shocking or notorious

Worksheet: Whatever happened to protest?

Comprehension

1. Why, in the eyes of this author, are Americans not obliged to support their government at a time of war? Why does he start with this point?
2. Explain, in your own words, what is meant by The Bush Doctrine.
3. In what different ways have Americans traditionally shown their disapproval of their governments' decision to go to war? You may go beyond the text if you wish.

Analysis

Choose *one* of the following tasks. Write 200–300 words.

1. Outline the current climate in the USA, as described by the author, and comment on it in the light of America's "proud record of debate and dissent" at a time of war.
2. Examine the function of the last section of the essay from line 76 onwards. How does the writer achieve the intended effect?

Composition

Choose *one* of the following tasks. Write a minimum of 200–300 words

1. Select one famous protestor you know of or admire and write an account of that person's life and achievements.
2. America should stop acting the interfering bully. Discuss this view.

Key: Whatever happened to protest?

Comprehension

1. *Why, in the eyes of this author, are Americans not obliged to support their government at a time of war? Why does he start with this point?*

It would be of help when answering this question

- to be able to define or quote from the **First Amendment** to the Constitution of the USA.
- to carefully read **all** the extract.

The reason the author believes that Americans are not obliged to do this is that the fundamental principle of the freedom of a person to choose to act according to his own beliefs and not have to follow the orders of a president is higher than the obligation to support your country at a time of war. Basically, the person comes before the country. **In other words**, as a political leader, you can't force your subjects to follow you to war just because you consider this to be the right thing to do. In addition to this, the First Amendment to the Constitution of the United States of America states that nobody can tell a person what to do in the areas of religion or politics. This means that all Americans are free to make up their own minds about whether or not they should support this president and the war he has lead their country into. The author begins his essay with this point in order to show that protest is justified and that moral right is on the side of the protesters once more. This allows him to also highlight the current mood in the USA at the moment.

2. *Explain, in your own words, what is meant by The Bush Doctrine.*

Keep in mind that

- although this answer can be very short it would better to write as much as you know of it, filling in the background as you go.
- above all else, however, you must put one particular phrase in the text into **your own words**.

The Bush Doctrine did not come into existence just because George Bush supports it. **In actual fact**, this is another name for the belief that leaders of countries, religions or ideologies are entitled to wage war, violate contracts, repudiate obligations and meddle in the affairs of their own citizens and others because their beliefs are superior to all others and justify their mission. It existed in the 19th century as much as it does now. In practical terms it means you hit the enemy before he hits you. Nowadays, **it is referred to** at a militaristic level as pre-emptive action or as this author calls it "anticipatory self-defence."

3. *In what different ways have Americans traditionally shown their disapproval of their governments' decision to go to war? You may go beyond the text if you wish.*

In order to get good marks here it is vital you

- read the text and gather the points needed for the answer.
- place the ways Americans have shown dissent in a **logical and structured order**.
- back up the points with **examples** you yourself can think of.
- introduce any other factors which are not referred to in the text.

For many years Americans believed in a policy of existing in splendid isolation from the rest of the world so any war they were going to get involved in would always be controversial. They have always found many different ways of voicing this disapproval. Americans have voted against war in parliament and they have refused to send soldiers to fight. Their authors, singers and poets, people such as Joan Baez and Bob Dylan, have spoken out against war, protestors have marched for peace, single individuals such as Cassius Clay and Robert Lowell have ended up in prison rather than go to war. In private they held discussions on the right thing to do and in public they have denounced the politicians who have waged war. Newspapers such as The Washington Post have taken anti-war stances; letter writers have vented their anger in letters to the editor. All these factors highlight the ways in which Americans have traditionally shown dissent.

Analysis

1. *Outline the current climate in the USA, as described by the author, and comment on it in the light of America's "proud record of debate and dissent" at a time of war.*

This question differs from the others in that you

- have to find the information in the text regarding the current climate in the USA.
- have to state your opinion on that. In other words say what you think of the current mood in America.
- may say whether you agree with the author on the matter.

The current climate is one the author finds extremely upsetting and troubling. Many people seem to believe that support for the president can not in any way be withheld. America is at war and the President needs help and support. People voice this opinion when they ask what else they would do but support the man. It would seem that this climate is not in keeping with America's tradition of dissent. The rest of the essay is spent showing how much discussion their normally is at a time like this. **In fact** the author sounds downright worried by the "imperial presidency" and this is something he sets out to change by reminding people of their duty to discuss and debate the current administration's policy. There is no doubt but we should be worried by the lack of criticism of the President's policies and the Bush Doctrine in general. The phrase is really only a horrible way of saying a leader can do whatever he likes and in view of the fact that such traits in Saddam Hussein were loudly criticised by successive American administrations it is a hypocritical belief. **If one takes the doctrine to its logical conclusion** then all leaders the world over have the right to go to war whenever they feel like it. And that, of course, is neither morally right nor a situation any of us in our sane minds could want.

2. *Examine the function of the last section of the essay from line 76 onwards. How does the writer achieve the intended effect?*

Ask yourself the following questions:

- What is in the section?
- What **effect has the section on the reader**?
- **What purpose** the section fulfils in the overall context of the essay?
- Is it **a turning point**? An **introduction**?
- Could it be classified as a **re-emphasising**? **A conclusion**?
- Does the author **define** something?
- **Does he substantiate a claim**? Confirm a fact?

This section, which consists of two short paragraphs, serves a double function. **On the one hand** it allows the writer to emphasise how frequently America has been to war in the last 100 years and how large a role dissent played then. **On the other hand**, it allows the writer to state his point of view once more and thus bring the essay to an appropriate conclusion. He begins the section by giving examples of the wars he remembers well e. g. the First World War, The Second World War as well as the fight in Vietnam and he reminds the reader of how horrible these combats were as well as how controversial and mistaken America's involvement in some of them was. With this point fresh in the reader's mind the author then goes on to praise the record of dissent in the USA and to leave the reader in no doubt as to where he stand on this matter. **He finishes with a final flourish** intended to impress and convince the reader of his argument. "Let us not restore the imperial presidency" is clever in that it is not only a statement of his beliefs but also an appeal to his readers to come round to his way of thinking and not listen to the rantings of their president.

Composition

1. *Select one famous protestor you know of or admire and write an essay on that person's life and achievements.*

The person you choose must be someone

- **you know a lot about**, e. g. life, background, achievements.
- you can point to and say "This man or woman is well-known for a protest action he or she carried out."
- you can place your person in a certain context, e. g. the times he or she lived in.

It was the early sixties and America was growing up. The rock 'n roll revolution, the advent of oral contraception, flower power and student movements meant things were changing forever. The death of John F. Kennedy was fresh in the minds of all Americans. Most of all the war in Vietnam was getting bloodier, costlier and more worrying. The government was drafting all the young men it could find to serve in Vietnam. There were many who did not believe in the war the government was waging but, apart from students, there were very few people prepared to do or say anything about it. In fact with the exception of the ban-the-bomb movement, protest was linked mainly to the Black struggle for equality.

At that time, 1964, a young boxer by the name of Cassius Clay had emerged on the world stage. After a 7th round knockout of world champion Sonny Liston, Clay became the new holder of the crown. Cassius Clay used his superior speed and punching power to overcome a tremendous opponent. The experts were left speechless. His hometown of Louisville, Kentucky beamed with pride. His parents became overnight celebrities. Later in the year he informed the world that he had joined the Nation of Islam (Black Muslims) and adopted the name of Muhammad Ali. Explaining his objections to the war and the importance of religion in his life, he then caused a furore by requesting "conscientious objector" status instead of reporting for the draft and probable military duty in Vietnam.

America, and the world, was stunned. This decision came at an awkward time in the history of America. His next four fights were held outside the United States. Ali was convicted of evading the draft and ended up in prison. This cost him his world title. Yet, despite the controversy, Ali stood by his new name and his adopted faith. With the benefit of hindsight we now know that it was one of the most famous and correct protests anyone ever made. Despite what many Americans thought at the time, Ali had right on his side but it was still a difficult thing for him to do. His conviction was eventually overturned by the US Supreme Court and time has granted Ali a special place in the history of protest. His major achievement was to speak out against something that was wrong and to show leadership to others at a time of crisis.

2. *America should stop acting the interfering bully. Discuss this view.*

There is a strong argument for this point of view but likewise, as we shall see, **one can find plenty of information to refute it**. America has been a powerful nation for over two hundred years. During this time, and increasingly of late, America has often portrayed itself as a land of liberty and democracy. **In the eyes of many** supporters of America it is a friendly giant, a land that has helped other countries stay free in the past and will continue to do so in the future. Look at the way Bill Clinton's foreign policy helped the peace process in Northern Ireland they say! Or the way America helped free Europe of the tyranny that was brought about by Adolf Hitler. Who freed the Jews in Dachau they ask. American troops of course. Whose money rebuilt Germany? American dollars naturally.

Lately, many Americans have been **carried away by** George W. Bush's speeches about America's new war, believing that the current attacks on Afghanistan, Iraq and Syria will provide a permanent solution to the threat of terrorist attacks. Yet neither this brainwashing propaganda, nor the national media's biased coverage of the current crisis, can mask the fact that the United States needs to rethink its foreign policy. In the eyes of a great many nations of the world America is a bully. Has in fact always been ever since the wealth of the land's resources started its huge growth. The Indians experienced this bully boy behaviour as did those who fought against invading American troops in Korea, Vietnam, Congo, Afghanistan, Iraq, Liberia and so on.

No matter what the current president wants people to believe, the terrorists who committed the atrocious acts of September 11 were not motivated by a desire to destroy human life on a large scale. Instead, they acted primarily on a political impetus, hoping to disrupt a country that has dominated world affairs ever since the end of the Cold War. **To be honest, I would be the first person to say** that it is not unreasonable for America to want such a major role in world affairs, but it must learn to step back. It is up to George W. Bush to engage a new foreign policy, one in which the United States plays a less involved role in world affairs. Such a move would reduce the United States' role in the world but it would also help America in the long run, for it would become a shining light of democracy, freedom, and justice. Just think of the respect America would then have earned.

The Next Assignment

In this century, the wealth and success of nations will depend like never before on the ability to produce and use knowledge. Universities have long been instrumental in generating knowledge and ideas. But in an increasingly globalized world, and in the face of rapid scientific change, they will need to think about a set of new challenges and how to best prepare their students for the coming decades.

It will be vital, as never before, for university graduates to have a grasp of foreign cultures and global issues. Before September 11, 2001, if you had asked the average American to name a remote country that matters little to the United States, the response might well have been Afghanistan. Today, it is clear that no country is so remote that it cannot affect our way of life. Universities, especially in the United States, will need to evolve to reflect the reality of interdependence, to educate more foreign students, to send more of their students abroad and to incorporate international perspectives in every area of study.

Universities will need to teach a new kind of literacy, defined not only by global awareness. They also need to grapple with the dilemmas posed by the accelerating pace of change brought on by scientific and technological advances. We are on the brink of once-in-human-history progress in combating disease through the application of modern science. Doctors will have at their disposal blood tests that will tell you with substantial predictive power how long you will live and from what diseases you are likely to suffer. The Internet and the application of information technology may well represent the most profound change in the way knowledge is disseminated since the printing press. We are close to understanding the first second of the history of the cosmos.

Beyond their contribution to scientific progress, universities are uniquely suited to grapple with the important ethical questions raised by modern science. This means that those who wish to be educated members of our society will need to understand something of science and technology. It may once have been acutely embarrassing to not know the names of five plays by Shakespeare but acceptable to not know the difference between a gene and a chromosome. This can no longer be the case. Institutions of higher learning have begun adapting to this reality, but they still have a long way to go.

As universities seek to meet the challenges of greater global integration and more advanced science, they will need to keep in mind the values that have been central to their success:

First, *a commitment to the pursuit of truth for its own sake.* Universities work best when they are driven by the authority of ideas, not the idea of authority; when they seek eternal truths, not transient reflections, and when students are taught not specific facts, but broad ways of thinking.

Second, *a commitment to excellence and diversity.* A century ago, Harvard was a place where New England gentlemen taught the sons of other New England gentlemen. Widening the circle from which we draw students and teachers while maintaining our rigorous standards has allowed us to be a more excellent university.

Third, *a commitment to constant challenge.* Universities have long been places where professors challenge their students, but the best of them have been places where students are encouraged to challenge their professors.

If universities adapted to the challenges of the new century while holding true to the values that have made them successful, they will fulfil their mission and serve society. For in the long run, it is new ideas and those who bring them forth and implement them that will shape our common destiny. 613 words

© Lawrence Summers, reprinted in Newsweek Special Issue Jan/Feb 2003

Worksheet: The Next Assignment

Comprehension

1. What factors, according to the author, make universities so important to society?
2. What arguments does the author put forward as to how universities should go about meeting the challenges of the next century?
3. Describe how the author uses language to convey his message.

Analysis

Choose *one* of the following tasks. Write 200–300 words.

1. Define, in precise terms, what the author means when he refers to "a new kind of literacy."
2. In former times how were universities different to the university of the 21st century? Go beyond the text in your answer.

Composition

Choose *one* of the following tasks. Write a minimum of 200–300 words.

1. You have been given the opportunity to do one year of your university course at a university in a foreign country. Write an essay outlining the country you would decide to go to and why, as well as the advantages and disadvantages of such a scheme.
2. Third-level Education – a privilege of the rich? Discuss.

Key: The Next Assignment

Comprehension

1. *What factors, according to the author, make universities so important to society?*

Keep the following in mind:
- You must search quite a bit for the answer to this question. It is not limited to any single part of the text.
- Read and underline the relevant points.
- You should come up with **at least three factors** if you hope to score well.

The first factor eluded to by the author concerns the contribution of universities to knowledge. **In the author's opinion** universities are places which help ideas circulate and come to the fore. Knowledge is in this way increased and society benefits. Universities are therefore crucial to a nation's success. Likewise, change **is directly linked to** universities as it is a product of their scientific research and technological developments. Universities are also important in that they help find solutions to ethical questions of the day which are frequently a source of worry in society. Finally, universities are important in that they plot the future of nations and the societies we live in.

2. *What arguments does the author put forward as to how universities should go about meeting the challenges of the next century.*

This is very much a question in which
- you have to put the author's ideas down on paper as you understand them.
- you should ask yourself what he is saying with regard to the university of the future.
- you should read the text from start to finish to find out how he makes his point.
- you will need **about four arguments** to score well.

There are a number of arguments put forward by the author with regard to this. The most important is that universities should not forget what made them successful in the first place. This includes having truth, excellence and commitment high on their list of priorities and values. It was this that made them great and this will keep universities great. **Secondly, and more specifically**, universities must educate more foreign students. In addition to this they must send more of their own students abroad. This swopping of students will help them meet global needs that now exist. They must also face up to and deal with the problems which ethical questions bring about. This is certainly true in the areas of science and technology. **Last but not least**, the universities of the future must incorporate an international viewpoint into each and every single course they offer. This, according to the author, is the way forward.

3. *Describe how the author uses language to convey his message.*

The first point to make is that this type of question appears frequently on exam papers. To answer it properly it is advisable

- to keep such **common stylistic devices** as alliteration, metaphors, repetition, similes, and contrast in mind and see if they are present in the text.
- to study **the style, the syntax and the grammar** used.
- to examine in particular his use of verbs, elevated choice of words, humour, wit, slang, hyperbole, sarcasm.
- to structure your answer and support the examples used with explanations as to their function.

The author of this text sets out to remind and convince the reader of the need for universities of the future to teach their students a new kind of literacy. The style he uses is polished and at times he uses **elevated language**. Syntax is likewise cut to meet a certain measure and he also makes deliberate use of a number of stylistic devices in the course of his essay. Let us take syntax first of all. There are few short sentences in this passage with many sentences being quite long especially when the author wants to show the reader the many different things a university of the future will have to do. Such sentences comprise of a list of measures the universities must undertake. Yet, at the end of the essay short sentences are used to stress certain points e. g. "Second, a commitment to excellence and diversity." Syntax then is used according to the message he is passing on to the reader. As far as style is concerned the author writes in a polished, accomplished, and comfortable way. A sentence such as "The Internet and the application of information technology may well represent the most profound change in the way knowledge is disseminated since the printing press." is proof of his ability to write in a formidable style which adds overall authority to what he is actually saying. It is his use of stylistic devices however which most catches the eye. **For example**, he repeats the phrase “a commitment to” three times at the end of the essay when he is hammering home to the reader what exactly it is that has made universities of the past important. **In addition** he turns words around in such eye-catching examples as “the authority of ideas, not the idea of authority” or “where professors challenge their students … students are encouraged to challenge their professors” Contrast is another device he uses when he says “eternal truths, not transient reflections” or later when he writes “specific facts, but broad ways of thinking”.

Analysis

1. *Define, in precise terms, what the author means when he refers to “a new kind of literacy.”*

In order to answer this question successfully you must

- use your own words as much as possible. To this end you should use your dictionary and get a definition of the word literacy.
- define the term accurately not just in itself but within the context of the extract.
- look and see how it fits in with the author's argumentation. This should lead you to a better understanding of the term.

As described in this text the new literacy the author refers to encompasses far more than the old definition of literacy. Literacy, **of course**, has traditionally meant the ability to read and write. Taken a step further it can refer to being extremely proficient in the use of language at all levels. **In former times** this would have indicated an ability to read and understand the works of Shakespeare and might have suggested a person who had studied Latin or Greek. The author defines literacy in new terms based on the changing world he sees around him. He believes that people who possess this new type of literacy will be able to understand other peoples and cultures as well as being fully up to date on current affairs at a global level. Likewise they will have a deep understanding of science, technological developments and the changing state of society. **As far as the author is concerned** the new role of universities in society is fundamentally linked to this new literacy and it is up to the universities to educate people towards this goal.

2. *In former times how were universities different to the university of the 21st century? Go beyond the text in your answer.*

The answer to this question is not fully to be had in the text itself. Therefore you must

- use your overall understanding and knowledge of the topic to score well.
- take a certain amount of your information from what the author says about the modern university of the future.

Due to the fact that this article is mainly about the future university rather than the university of the past there is not an awful amount of information given directly to the reader on how universities used to be. The author does of course tell us that universities were places which taught people from the upper class. Note the author's words "New England gentlemen taught the sons of other New England gentlemen." Third-level education then was not for the poor – nowadays this has changed to a considerable degree. **As a result** of the fact that some working class people aspire to – and succeed in getting to – university the numbers attending have increased and this is a significant development. The other difference the author points out is that in former times work by Shakespeare and other genres of literature were on an even plane with science, medicine and so on. Latin and Greek were considered highly important. The third difference is the fact that universities did not have a global reach like they now have. They served the needs of regional education and rarely looked beyond their own shores. Other differences which I would point out include the fact that universities have become more image conscious, are run on business lines, and have closer links nowadays with other parts of society than they used to have. Generally-speaking they are quite different places to what they used to be.

Composition

1. *You have been given the opportunity to do one year of your university course at a university in a foreign country. Write an essay outlining the country you would decide to go to and why, as well as the advantages and disadvantages of such a scheme.*

For this essay it is important

- that you **know something about the country you choose**, e. g. background information on the education system, perhaps even the city and university in question.
- that you clearly describe both the advantages and disadvantages of the scheme.

If I was taking part in such a scheme I think my choice of country would be Ireland. While countries such as Britain or America immediately come to mind, a smaller country has its advantages for a person leaving their native land for the first time. Such a break is not always easy and it involves leaving home. Therefore, my first reason would be to go to a place which is not anonymous and cold, not a huge city or metropolis, but to go to a place which might be a large town or middle-sized city. There I think I could make friends and get to know people well.

Ireland has the name of being a friendly place and in recent times has experienced a great deal of change and economic boom. It has a system of education that is well known for being quite progressive. The university I would choose would be either the University of Galway or that in Cork. My reason for doing so would be that both these universities have long traditions in the study of folklore and that is one of my core subjects. They are both close to areas where two languages are spoken and this is a theme in which I hope to major.

This kind of scheme has a lot of advantages for someone like me. I get the chance to travel, to study at another university, to see a new way of life, to make friends with people I would not normally expect to meet. It is excellent for my studies in that I come under the influence of new professors and new schools of thought.

The major disadvantage I see is that of moving home. I will have to leave my parents and pay rent. It will not always be possible to have the comforts I am used to and I will also have major expenses in transporting my belongings. Otherwise it's a great idea and I'm dying to get going!

2. *Third-level Education – the privilege of the rich?*

This statement

- Sets out to provoke you into looking at it from both sides.
- Requires at least **three arguments** to support your thesis.
- Allows you to be in favour or against this but you must support your claim with evidence.
- Expects you to look at the side of the discussion you do not agree with.
- Demands you come to a **general conclusion**. That can be a conclusion, if you wish, which does not come down on one side or the other but takes a middle ground position.

This theme **rears its ugly head** whenever a government considers altering or raising university fees. The fact of the matter is that when a government implements such a move and entry to college becomes dearer it very quickly eliminates university education as an option for thousands of students. Some courses become so expensive that only the rich can afford them. In Britain and Australia to take two examples public funding for university education has progressively shrunk in recent times. Public universities have been forced to become more reliant on the corporate sector and student fees. Consequently, courses have been cut, the integrity and independence of research threatened and a university education put beyond the reach of many potential students. **It is my opinion that** education is a privilege of the rich and is becoming more and more so as governments tighten their belts. **Can that be right I ask you?** Having opened up the prospect of university education to the working class in particular do we just cruelly take it away again?

It has often been remarked that as far back as the 1920s George Bernard Shaw wrote an essay pointing out the outrageous injustice of university education facilities being built with public money and then being accessible only to the very rich. **This still holds true today**. Shaw also noted that this process ensured that the nation's development was being stunted by a system in which the collective intellect of only 16 percent of the population was cultivated. In the 1970s, in some countries, university fees were abolished, only to be re-introduced later on. All this leads to countries underperforming. What we need once and for all is that university education becomes free the world over.

If this does not happen many students will continue to be forced into debt or to drop out of their courses. I have seen that happen to friends of mine whose parents are unemployed. My father, a doctor, has no such problems paying my fees. And the world will be a poorer place all round if we allow this kind of injustice to go on. **I suggest** not only investing more money into free university education but that big business should have to pay a new university tax which would be a percentage of their annual profits. After all business wants skilled workers – if that's the case it should have to contribute something to the cost.

To conclude then I think that education is and always has been something for rich rather than for poorer people. The only way we can change this is to force governments to make higher education free to all who want to use it.

British diplomacy has finally met its Waterloo

Tony Blair looks older, greyer and full of strain. This is usually blamed on two much travel and too little sleep, yet that is not the real reason. After all, Tony Blair is fit and in the prime of life, doing one of the most interesting jobs in the world that stimulates even when it stresses. Though he may need and deserve a holiday, he is not looking haggard because he is knackered. The cares of office are oppressing his spirits, but only because a crucial area of policy has gone wrong.

Diplomacy has gone wrong. Everything was supposed to have turned out differently. After 11 September, the Prime Minister's calculations rapidly caught up with his immediate response. He saw a great diplomatic opportunity. Britain could constrain American unilateralism by proving that international institutions could work – including the EU – and that the US could secure redress of grievance within international law and a framework of alliances. Mr Blair also believed that he could convince the Europeans of the Americans' case, thus demonstrating the usefulness of the special relationship and its compatibility with EU membership.

He set about this task with optimism and enthusiasm. He tried, he talked, he failed. As a result, British foreign policy is even more frayed than the PM's features.

In the Foreign Office itself, and especially among those with EU responsibilities, there is alarm and despondency. The FO has finally stopped denying that the Government's Euro-diplomacy has been hit by a Cruise missile, and is beginning to recognise that years of effort have been wasted. Our diplomats are dismayed by some of the thinking aloud that is now coming out of Paris and Berlin. "De Gaulle was right," they are arguing. "We cannot trust the British. In any crisis, they will always side with the Americans. That is even true under Mr Blair, who has always assured us that he is a Europhile. If this Prime Minister cannot bring Britain into Europe, who can? So if the EU is ever to have an effective diplomacy, we have to devise new structures that exclude the Anglo Saxons."

That sort of talk horrifies the Foreign Office, and Mr Blair. But it is not clear what they can do about it. From a Franco/German perspective, anti-British feeling is hardly an irrational response to recent events. The skill with which the UK has disrupted the EU will not endear us to our Continental partners. Mr Blair would like to regain Europe's trust, but how?

The Prime Minister is much less happy about trading Europe for America than many in his own party darkly suspect. Given their differences in outlook and background, the Bush/Blair friendship is a tribute to both men's geniality and charm. But there is no profound meeting of minds. George Bush is not only more intelligent than most Europeans recognise; he is also much colder and more driven. This is a man with very few close friends and very strong ideological certainties.

It is a recurring source of surprise to Mr Bush that he finds it easy to collaborate with a non-conservative. At moments of overreach even by their standards, Number 10 spin doctors have occasionally suggested that Mr Blair is the leading intellectual partner in the relationship. That could never be true. Mr Bush, who does not lack intellectual self-confidence, would never dream of deferring to a non-conservative politician. When Tony Blair agrees with the President, Mr Bush inwardly congratulates him from escaping from his dubious political origins. When he holds back, the President assumes that Mr Blair is succumbing to those origins, or to his party.

Mr Bush, who is surprisingly well-informed about the European debate in Britain, cannot understand why any sensible Brit would choose the EU over the special relationship. Mr Blair thought, as he so often thinks, that he could avoid choice by embracing both the apparent rivals. Over Iraq, he found, as he will find increasingly, that conflict was inescapable.

So it will continue. Soon, (...) Mr Blair will find himself confronted by Israel/Palestine, another situation in which the contending parties are irreconcilable. I am not referring to the Israelis and Palestinians; over time, their disagreements could be reconciled. But the early conflict will be between the Americans and the EU. The EU will want a role in the Middle East. The US will be determined to exclude it.

The Bush administration is now ready to override many of its visceral instincts and to pursue the goal of a Palestinian state. Britain could play an important role in this, but only on our own. If we came as part of an EU package, we would be disregarded in Washington. Any European involvement would only antagonise the Americans and would be exploited by Israeli irreconcilables. Yet the EU will try to insist on a say and might even hope to pressurise the British into helping.

This will not succeed. Tony Blair has no choice. Even if it means snubbing the EU, he will have to assist the Americans. Yet it will be an irony if Britain's involvement in a Palestinian peace process, a long-desired goal of the EU and the British Europhiles, will also complete the destruction of Mr Blair's European credentials.
873 words

© *The Independent, March 24, 2003*

Annotations
knackered (line 5): very tired, exhausted

Worksheet: British diplomacy has finally met its Waterloo

Comprehension

1. Give Tony Blair's reasons for cooperating with the United States of America. To what extent have his hopes been fulfilled?
2. How have the EU partners mentioned in the text reacted to British involvement in the war?
3. What is the nature of the personal and political relationship between Blair and Bush as portrayed in the text.

Analysis

Choose *one* of the following tasks (write 200–300 words) or take the translation.

1. What danger does the author sees for Tony Blair's position in the future?
2. Analyse the two cartoons you see here. If you had to choose one of these to accompany the article you have just read which one would you choose. Give reasons.

© Peter Schrank/The Independent

© Peter Kornherr, Dorfen

Translation

Translate the following text into good German or choose *one* of the analysis tasks.

... America through the Bush Doctrine is now proposing to – albeit surreptitiously – resurrect and implement Manifest Destiny on a global scale, a policy that has always had horrific consequences for the selected 'enemy' and results in lasting enmity and resentment against the 'victor.' Instead of eliminating terrorism the Bush Doctrine and a policy of Manifest Destiny will, in fact, breed more terrorism. Throughout history the notion of Manifest Destiny has implied entitlement by leaders of countries, religions or ideologies to wage war, violate contracts, repudiate obligations and meddle in the affairs of their own citizens and others because their Deity sanctions their mission. Religion has been an integral part of man's customs and traditions from before the beginning of Empire and the appearance of the God-kings. The ambitious, ruthless and savvy routinely exploited and still do – the ignorant and illiterate masses with claims that their actions and destiny were ordained and sanctioned by God.

© 2003 by Errol Nelson. Source: http://www.secondmagnacarta.com

Composition

Choose *one* of the following tasks. Write a minimum of 200–300 words.

1. Letter to the Editor: War in Iraq
   As the mother or father of a young British soldier about to go to war you have been asked by the Guardian newspaper to write a letter to Tony Blair explaining why you are against the war in Iraq.
2. E-Mail Reply: Prospects for a United Europe.
   You and your fellow students are exchanging e-mails with pen pals at your American exchange school in preparation for a summer visit to the United States. One morning you receive the following question at the end of an e-mail from one American student. "Most people here say the Europeans will never form a United Europe. What do you say?" Write a reply to your friend in which, among other things, you answer this question of the possibility of a United Europe.

Key: British diplomacy has finally met its Waterloo

Comprehension

1. *Give Tony Blair's reasons for cooperating with the United States of America. To what extent have his hopes been fulfilled?*

This question demands you: Look at **all** the reasons Blair had for cooperating with the USA in order to answer it fully. There are at least **four** such reasons and you should mention each one.

Tony Blair had a number of reasons for cooperating with the United States of America. **First and foremost** among these was the great diplomatic chance he saw, after the attack on the Twin Towers, for Britain to act as a go-between in dealings between the EU and the USA. He imagined he would, as British Prime Minister, be able to put the brakes on American unilateralism and on American policies towards Iraq. He felt he could show that cross border institutional bodies such as the EU do work and that America would be able to bring those responsible for Sept 11 to court using international law and alliances. He in particular thought that cooperating with the United States would allow him to convince other European countries of the American argument and the usefulness of the special relationship between Britain and the USA. His hopes in this respect have not been fulfilled. He has tried hard, entered into many rounds of exhausting discussions but he has failed and British foreign policy is in a mess.

2. *How have the EU partners mentioned in the text reacted to British involvement in the war?*

To answer this question properly be sure to

- read the full text before starting your answer. Sometimes the answer to a question is not to be found in one section of a text but in different parts of it.
- identify the partners involved in the course of your answer.
- ask yourself have the partners reacted in a similar way.

Put in a nutshell the EU partners have reacted with dismay and anger to British involvement in the war. The author refers to the fact that the other EU partners, in this case France and Germany, have all suffered a loss of trust towards Britain. As far as they are concerned Britain cannot be trusted and is always likely to take the side of America in such a crisis. They are extremely disappointed in Blair himself who they had previously regarded as a Europhile and now consider that any future EU structures will have to be erected without the British. This is likely to mean a closer Franco-German alliance than has existed up to now. In general the disruption that recent events have caused has led to strong anti-British feelings among the EU partners and Blair will have a hard job winning back their trust.

3. *What is the nature of the personal and political relationship between Blair and Bush as portrayed in the text?*

As outlined in the text this is a personal and political relationship of convenience rather than one based on close friendship. The author explains it as being the result of both men's ability to get on with, and charm, other people. They are in fact very different in attitudes and background. Bush is a man with a cold personality and is very driven, believing strongly in all he stands for. The relationship between the two men is not one in which, as has sometimes been said, Blair is the partner with the stronger intellect. This is not a meeting of minds but a political partnership in which George Bush has shown himself very well up on European matters. In many ways one gets the sense from the author's article, both from his description of the relationship and from Blair's unfulfilled hopes, that it is a relationship in which Blair bit off a little more than he originally thought he could chew.

Analysis

1. *What danger does the author see for Tony Blair's position in the future?*

Basically **Blair is faced with a straightforward choice** – either he goes with America or the EU. The desire to solve the problems in Palestine means that Blair will have to decide whether or not he is going to exclude the EU from the process because otherwise his relationship with America will suffer. If, on the other hand, he sides with George Bush and America he runs the risk of damaging Britain's position within the European Community. This is the plight Blair faces and according to the author Blair will almost certainly have to help the Americans. Doing that and not offending the Europeans is where the real danger lies for Tony Blair. He has got himself into a no-win situation, and regardless of the course he chooses to pursue,

Britain and Blair himself will be the losers in a process that is of the Prime Minister's own making. Although it is not directly stated the possibility that Blair would fall from power cannot be excluded. Any change to Blair's foreign policy clearly holds great danger for his position as British leader. the phrase 'a-no-win-situation' sums the position up.

2. *Analyse the two cartoons you see here. If you had to choose one of these to accompany the article you have just read which one would you choose. Give reasons.*

When analysing a cartoon you should ask yourself:

- Who is in the cartoon and what size are the characters and figures used?
  What is happening?
  Is the background simple or complicated?
- What **symbols** are used and what do the symbols represent?
  How do the symbols help convey the message of the cartoon?
- What **bias**, if any, is evident in the cartoon?
  Who looks nice, ugly, nasty, stupid?
  What facial features are used to convey expressions e. g. happiness, meanness, annoyance?
  Has the cartoonist taken sides?
- What is the cartoon/comic strip saying?
  What ideas does the cartoonist want you to think about?
  Does the cartoon express a serious message?
  Is it just entertainment?
- Has the cartoonist used **headings, speech balloons or captions** to help to get ideas across?
- In this case you must analyse what you see in the cartoon (objects, people, the way they look or are dressed, other significant details such as what they are doing)
- Select the points that the cartoon has in common with the text.

The first observation to make is that both cartoons deal with the same general theme. Both make use of a simple but effective background. Both make use of symbols to convey their message e. g. the statue and the French boat. Of the two cartoons I would use the one showing a pompous-looking George Bush standing on top of a statue as accompanying material for the article. My reason for doing this would be that the main theme of the article is the manner in which Bush now has Tony Blair in his pocket and how

Blair's foreign policy has gone awry, leaving him as a small player on a big stage. The cartoon also brings across the idea of America being the dominant partner in the special relationship and of Bush in particular having control of Blair. The cartoon cleverly shows Bush towering, Statue of Liberty-like, over the world and this also mirrors an aspect of the article. In fact the cartoonist has cleverly raised Bush's hand in order to give the reader the idea that Bush is not just a leader in search of freedom but a dictator as well. The use of the upper half of the globe serves to locate the dispute and conveys the idea of a new world order with the USA reigning supreme. The presence of a large amount of black helps hit home how serious a situation this is. The other cartoon highlights a completely different aspect of the debate – namely the French resistance to America. It plays on the word veto and shows the French Prime Minister sticking a veto sign at the boat driven by a downcast George Bush and a terrified Tony Blair. This cartoon makes more use of language – "victoire" – than the other and in some ways it contains far more information than the other. Yet it does not reflect the main theme of the article.

Translation

... im Zuge der Bush'schen Glaubenslehre schlägt Amerika jetzt – wenn auch versteckt – vor, ‚Manifest Destiny' wieder ins Leben zu rufen und global einzusetzen; eine Politik, die schon immer entsetzliche Folgen für den ausgewählten ‚Feind' mit sich brachte und zu nachhaltiger Feindseligkeit und Missgunst gegen den ‚Sieger' führt. Anstatt dem Terrorismus ein Ende zu setzen, werden die Bush'sche Glaubenslehre und eine Politik des ‚Manifest Destiny' in Wirklichkeit mehr Terrorismus hervorbringen. In der Geschichte wurde von der Idee von ‚Manifest Destiny' das Recht der Führer von Ländern, Religionen oder Ideologien abgeleitet, Krieg zu führen, Verträge zu verletzen, Verpflichtungen zu leugnen und sich in die Angelegenheiten der eigenen und anderer Bürger einzumischen, weil ihre ‚Gottheit' ihre Mission unterstützte. Die Religion war ein wesentlicher Teil der menschlichen Sitten und Traditionen schon vor dem Anfang des Reichsgedankens und dem Aufkommen der Vorstellung von der Gottgleichheit von Herrschern. Mit der Behauptung, ihre Handlungen und ihr Schicksal seien von Gott bestimmt und gewollt, beuteten die Ehrgeizigen, Unbarmherzigen und Schlauen die ungebildeten Massen unentwegt aus – und sie tun es immer noch.

Composition

1. *As the mother or father of a young British soldier about to go to war you have been asked by the Guardian newspaper to write a letter to Tony Blair explaining why you are against the war in Iraq.*

When answering this question do not forget to
- place yourself in the position such a mother finds herself in (**hopes**, **feelings**, **worries**).
- find good arguments against the war.
- use **historical and political** information in your letter.
- use the **formal aspects** of a letter (Address, date, greeting, etc.).

33 Walton Road
Manchester
23 March 2003

Dear Mr Blair,

My son, Alan, joined the army two years ago because he wished to serve his country. Neither his father nor I tried to dissuade him as we are proud both of our son and of his patriotism. Yet, as I write, he is getting ready to leave for Iraq and it is very hard for me to feel anything but cynicism about the political decisions you and George Bush are taking. America wants war – of that there is no doubt. Everything else is window dressing. To your great shame history will record that the stance the British government is taking is a cowardly one.
How many innocent Iraqis will die in the next few weeks Mr Blair? How many invaluable buildings and treasures will be bombed, looted or destroyed? Will my son kill or be killed in the name of what you call freedom? We are all aware of the menace of Saddam's regime. We know he has killed, maimed and raped people within his own country. He may – or may not – have weapons of mass destruction. However, none of these factors justify the decision of pre-emptive action which you and your American partner are taking. If that were the case then any power any where in the world would be justified in attacking another. George Bush – as we now know – is every bit the bully Saddam is. His interests are a long way from those of a free and democratic world. Why, Mr Blair, can you not see that the long term damage – not to mind the short term destruction – of your alliance with this man will take decades to erase?

As a Labour supporter I find it depressing to recall the jubilation caused by the 1997 election. You have ruined our hopes for a just society in attempting to be a player on the world stage and aligning yourself with George Bush. It does not seem to trouble you that US firms have already been given the contracts for rebuilding Iraq, nor are you prepared to admit that what lies behind this war is American imperialism and a lust for control of a new world order. Your actions are sowing the seeds of further conflict in the Middle East and you do this without ever wondering how we are supposed to control the post-war situation in Iraq. Have you forgotten, Mr Blair, the brutal stupidity of decades of British policy in Northern Ireland? Do you honestly believe Iraqis will want my son and other British soldiers patrolling the streets of Baghdad? A woman in our street lost her eldest boy to an IRA sniper bullet. If the same should happen to our child then may God forgive you, Mr Blair. I will not.
Yours, in the hope you may change your mind,

Mary Parlour

2. *Prospects for a United Europe.*
You and your fellow students are exchanging e-mails with pen pals at your American exchange school in preparation for a summer visit to the United States. One morning you receive the following question at the end of an e-mail from one American student. "Most people here say the Europeans will never form a United Europe. What do you say?" Write a reply to your friend in which, among other things, you answer this question of the possibility of a United Europe.

In the case of this question you
- may use a more informal style than with a letter.
- should base your opinion on concrete evidence and examples.
- might include a bit of humour if possible.
- try and think of a strong point or punch line as your conclusion.

Hi Bruce,

Thanks for your mail. No news here – hopefully it won't be long now until we can start packing for our trip. As to your question about Europe – that's a hard one!

Europe is both a united and divided place. Dad says Europe meant nothing to him when he was young and now it does. The growth of the EU has helped a great deal in this respect. Take integration of the EU economies for instance. Did you know that this process will create a single market of more than 360 million people? That is certainly going to unite Europeans more and more.

On the other hand we speak a heck of a lot of languages over here as you know from your stay with us last summer. These languages come from different cultures and there is no doubt but that the Germans, French and Italians don't always get on with each other. Have you ever seen the Eurovision Song Contest? It's a howl! All countries put forward a song in the competition so that they can vote against the countries they don't like. The Austrians give the Germans no votes, the Irish hate giving the English anything and it's the same with the Greek and the Turks, the English and French etc.

At the moment, although the war in Iraq is over, the political crisis that it created is still alive. Most of Europe did not like George Bush's policies but that did not unite governments here. There is no common foreign policy for example. France and Germany are committed to creating a new military alliance, Britain places its special relationship with the United States above loyalty to its European partners, Poland openly wishes to promote the U.S. line in an expanded EU. And so on. Over the past decade, we have heard loads of talk about "common European values" – but these common values didn't count for much during the Iraq crisis. And when discussing the design of the euro bank notes, officials in Brussels decided against using the faces of historical personalities – they were afraid that one country's historical figures would be offensive to the population of another.

Nevertheless it's great to have the Euro – we go on holiday a lot and these days we don't have to change currency for most of the places we visit. I can't really say if there will ever be a united Europe the way there is a USA. We are coming together in a lot of ways but sometimes we seem as far apart as ever. I'm in favour of unity but a lot of the magic of Europe lies in its differences and variety. Now that you have asked the question you have set me thinking: Do you think the United States could ever break up?

Take care,
Stefan

Monarchy Prince Charles, a victim of monarchists' cruelty

Because of the silliness of monarchy, he has repeatedly been placed in situations for which he is entirely unsuitable

Republicans are often accused of hating the Royal Family, while monarchists claim they "love" Elizabeth and Charles Windsor. Yet, in truth, it is the monarchists who are putting the Windsors through hell and we republicans who want to set them free to live a normal life. When the in-house investigation into the on-going farce at St James's Palace is released tomorrow, we will all be provided with another vivid illustration of this.

All the available evidence suggests that Charles Windsor is an unintelligent man who, in a kinder world, would not be placed in a managerial role of any kind. So, of course, the monarchists' decision to put him in charge of more than 300 servants where he can rule unchallenged – indeed, where everybody tells him how jolly clever and good all his ideas are – has ended in disaster.

... Because of the irrational nature of monarchy, Charles has been placed repeatedly – and pitilessly – in situations like this. Despite the best education money can buy, he achieved derisory A-level results, but was still admitted to Trinity College, Cambridge, solely because of who his mother was. Predictably, his degree was a belly-flop. He then went on to be almost comically incompetent in the navy. He couldn't master navigation for the life of him (a pretty fundamental skill when you're at sea), but equally the authorities couldn't punish his failures in the way they would with anybody else. As the Naval Secretary to the Ministry of Defence wrote: "The thought of Court Martialling the heir to the throne for a navigational error is good nightmare material." In the end, he had to be given multiple intensive courses until eventually he was receiving one-to-one tuition. Like Forrest Gump, he has wandered through life inadequate at everything, yet being lauded as though he were able.

Charles himself is not to blame. This is all the fault of the ridiculous institution of monarchy that has denied him the opportunity to find a job that suits his limited talents: working as a gardener, perhaps. (Charles is a horrible symbol of the fact that in addition to having very limited upward class mobility, we have almost no downward class mobility at all. In a meritocracy, he would probably fail – but instead, class ringfences him from that possibility). No wonder Charles is deluded. A friend of his told the gossip columnist Nigel Dempster that "he lives in an isolation ward of flattery. He goes to Hollywood and is told he's handsome. He swaps jokes with a comic genius like

Peter Sellers and the other Goons, and they fall down laughing. He boffs a woman once, and she tells him he's the greatest lover she's ever had ... The best education in the world can't defend you against sycophancy on that scale." This process – which is inherent to the cruel institution of monarchy – has warped Charles in innumerable ways, as it would any of us.

But, I hear you cry, doesn't Charles make learned speeches to academic audiences? Didn't he deliver one of the Reith lectures? How can he be stupid? Yet our soon-to-be-emperor has no intellectual clothes. Everything he touches – from his unsuccessful "model villages" to his personal staff – swiftly falls apart. His speeches are, by and large, cobbled-together nonsense received with a politeness based on his position rather than their quality. Even Charles's closest aides admit that all too often he simply spouts whatever the last person to whisper in his ear has said. His very sympathetic biographer Jonathan Dimbleby admits that his aides "were uncomfortable with his tendency to reach instant conclusions on the basis of insufficient thought". Edward Adeane, Charles's private secretary for many years, was deeply disturbed by the fact that "Charles was extraordinarily easy to lead by the nose". These are understatements.

The quality of his judgement can be seen in the mentors he has chosen for himself throughout his life. Look, for example, at the late Laurens van der Post. Charles revered Van der Post as a guru. He wined and dined him, and made great efforts to boost Van der Post's public standing, and even chose him as William's godfather. As Van der Post's distinguished official biographer JDF Jones puts it: "For 20 years, they shared the most intimate conversations and correspondence. Charles even told him about his dreams." Yet Van der Post was, as Jones says, "a compulsive fantasist". He intoxicated Charles with his tales of the "noble savages" who lived in the Kalahari. These condescending myths had long since been discredited by anthropologists (something Charles really ought to have known since he studied the subject, at least nominally, at university), but Van der Post repeated them as though they reflected his own experiences. (...) Most people spotted that Van der Post was a charlatan at 50 paces; Charles lapped up this gibberish.

Yet the monarchists still encourage the exploitation of Charles by people like this. It is Charles who suffers, because he is allowed to entertain delusions about his own intellect. When it was revealed last year that Charles bombards busy government ministers with his incoherent ramblings – and becomes extremely petulant if they do not respond promptly – they said that he was "performing his civil duty". His office announced that he "will not be diverted from using the authority of his position to speak out across a range of public issues". But what authority does his position have? Why on earth should a hereditary position have any authority at all? To allow him to entertain this belief is to encourage madness.

We even allow him to display hypocrisy on a staggering scale without positing out that he is making himself into a national joke. Remember: this is a man who preaches fuel conservation yet drives one of the greatest fuel-wasters in the world, a Bentley – or rather, three of them. This is a man who took a trip to the USA to inspect urban slums and spent half the trip playing polo. This is a man who preaches about agricultural traditionalism but was quite happy to shut down his own "model farms" so that he could make an extra few quid by "rationalising" the Duchy of Cornwall.

The revelations tomorrow will just be another reminder that monarchy has placed Charles Windsor in a situation for which he is entirely unsuitable. How could genes determine your suitability to be head of state? It is time to end the cruelty of the monarchists and release Charles to live in the countryside he loves and marry Camilla without fretting about the Church of England – and to introduce a sensible way of selecting our future head of state. Elections, anyone? 1107 words

© *The Independent, March 12, 2003*

Annotations

Reith Lectures (line 4): Inaugurated in 1948 to mark the contribution made to public service broadcasting by Lord Reith, each year the BBC invites a leading figure to deliver a series of lectures on radio to advance debate about significant issues of contemporary interest.

sycophancy (line 37): the use of flattery to win favours

Worksheet: Monarchy Prince Charles, a victim of monarchists' cruelty

Comprehension

1. How well has Prince Charles' education prepared him for a position of responsibility?
2. The author refers to "the ridiculous institution of monarchy". What disadvantages has this institution brought to Charles' life?
3. In what way, and for what reasons, should the position of head of state in Britain be changed according to the text?

Analysis

Choose *one* of the following tasks (write 200–300 words) or take the translation.

1. Explain why the text does not hold Prince Charles personally responsible for his failures? Give reasons why you agree or do not agree with this analysis?
2. How would you describe the Prince's overall character and his relationships with other people as shown in this article?

Translation

Translate the following text into good German or choose *one* of the analysis tasks.

Why the Queen drags us all down

... Writing about the royal family's foibles is, for me, a novelty. Ten days ago, I was about to resign from the Campaign for an Elected Head of State because of its attitude towards the Windsors' private lives, as revealed in the Panorama investigation of Camilla Parker Bowles's prospects of becoming queen. The simulated meeting of the campaign's committee showed an intolerably cynical approach to the business of promoting a republic. Professor Stephen Haseler, the chairman, announced that the personal conduct of the Prince of Wales must be exploited in the drive to end the hereditary monarchy. My arguments in favour of an elected head of state have always been built around the inadequacy of the institution, not the shortcomings of the individuals. Of course, I accepted that the heredity principle is based on the notion of a genetically distinct family, with everything that family does – in private as well as public –

providing evidence of its suitability to rule. But I was against the monarchy because it embodied the idea of a social hierarchy and encouraged the nation to look back instead of forward, not because the heir to the throne made childishly prurient telephone calls.

© Roy Hattersly, November 11, 2002, The Guardian

Composition

Choose *one* of the following tasks. Write a minimum of 200–300 words.

1. As a supporter of constitutional monarchy in Britain you have been asked by the editor of the Times to write a short article outlining the reasons why Britain should retain a monarch as well as the reforms needed to stop the constitutional monarchy becoming a thing of the past.
2. Choose one famous king, queen or member of a royal family whose life you consider to have been a good example of why there should not be a monarchical head of state in England. Write an essay on monarchy in which you highlight the failings of your chosen monarch and compare the position of the current queen to that of the German Bundestag President.

Key: Monarchy Prince Charles, a victim of monarchists' cruelty

Comprehension

1. *How well has Prince Charles' education prepared him for a position of responsibility?*

   In point of fact those responsible for Prince Charles' education tried very hard to prepare him well for a position of responsibility. We are told that Charles got the best education money can buy. In addition he went on to Trinity College, Cambridge, where he received further tuition. In other areas such as seamanship he got private instruction and all of this because he was a member of the Royal family. Nevertheless, as a grown man, he is still unable for a position of responsibility and his educational performance is not one he can look back on with pride. His A-level results were very poor and his degree at college is described by the author of this article as a "bellyflop". When he joined the navy he was found to be completely incompetent and made so many errors that any other ordinary seaman might have been court-martialled. Prince Charles's education has therefore not prepared him very well for a position of responsibility though this has been far more due to the Prince's shortcomings as a student than to the failures within the educational system he experienced. He was a poor student at many different stages of his education. In reality the Prince received a far longer education than a person with his exam results would normally receive but that still has not helped make him a person suited to a managerial role.

2. *The author refers to "the ridiculous institution of monarchy". What disadvantages has this institution brought to Charles' life?*

   The institution of monarchy has brought many disadvantages to the Prince's life. The first and most obvious disadvantage is that he has gone through life being treated differently to everybody else. Although not a very bright person he is constantly praised and allowed to pass exams not because of his performance but because of who his mother is. People tell him he is very bright when in reality he is not. Secondly, the monarchy has placed him in managerial positions to which he is just not suited. This is most obvious from the trouble is St James's Palace where he is in charge of 300 people. The text suggests he would make a good gardener. Thirdly, because Charles is the future monarch, he feels he has to speak out on a range of public matters when in actual fact all this amounts to is a well-known man rambling boringly on about a whole lot of different topics. The institution of the monarchy has also caused him to believe he has a right to be treated differently and he gets very annoyed when he does not get quick answers to his letters to politicians. Above all else the monarchy has left Charles unable to marry the woman he loves. As he is the future head of the Anglican Church of England this has meant he is not free to marry Camilla and this is another example of how the monarchy has handed Charles a life that in many ways is completely wrong for him.

3. *In what way, and for what reasons, should the position of head of state in Britain be changed according to the text?*

   The author of this text believes that the monarchy is bad for England. As a result he suggests replacing the means of selecting a head of state. He favours holding elections which would lead to a democratic head of state instead of a king or queen who gets the position by right of birth. The reasons he gives for this are manifold. First of all he says that the current Prince of Wales is not suited to the task and should be doing some other job e. g. that of gardener. In actual fact the monarchy is not only a bad idea but is also cruel to a person such as Prince Charles. The author uses this example to argue that genes cannot determine a person's suitability for a position such as head of state. The monarchy he says does not make sense and therefore the head of state should be elected by the people. Having a monarch as head of state is basically the same as having someone with no authority as your leader. In a number of ways the author emphasises that if you have not been elected to a position you are not entitled to it. For the sake of Prince Charles and the country in general it would be better to have an elected head of state.

Analysis

1. *Explain why the text does not hold Prince Charles personally responsible for his failures? Give reasons why you agree or do not agree with this analysis?*

When answering this question keep in mind that

- this question is a broad one and you must search the whole text for the answer.
- you should begin your answer with why the author thinks the Prince is not responsible.
- if you are going to agree or disagree with the analysis you must provide reasons for doing so.

The text argues that Prince Charles cannot be held responsible for the situation he finds himself in. It is not his fault that others praise him for things where no praise is warranted. The author puts the blame here on the institution of monarchy itself. If Charles is deluded it is because others delude him, if Charles cannot work as a gardener it is because the monarchy expects something else of him. If Charles cannot manage 300 people it is because he is not suited to this task. The author comes back **time and time again** to the madness and cruelty of the monarchy as a political system and this is why he does not hold the Prince responsible.

I consider much of this argument to be flawed. While fully agreeing that Charles is a victim of the family he has been born into, I think that to put the failures in his life down to this alone is a cop-out. Prince Charles, like all of us, is able to make choices. He could choose to do something else with his life but he does not. He could say he has no intention of becoming king yet he does not do that. Likewise, driving a Bentley while at the same time promoting fuel conservation or playing polo while visiting the poor are all his own decisions. They reveal a hypocritical person, a man who likes much of the benefits that go with being the Prince of Wales. His failures in life may have been highlighted and even partly caused by his position but **I do not agree with the author when he says** it's all the monarchy's fault. Prince Charles could change his own life if he really wanted to – the reality is that he is well aware of the benefits he has because he is a member of the Royal family.

2. *How would you describe the Prince's overall character and his relationships with other people as shown in this article?*

   The Prince comes across as a stupid and helpless individual who basically hasn't a clue about any thing. Useless at school, helped through university, guided through the navy he is a man of little character and many faults. The choice of mentors he made, the speeches he cobbles together and the life-style he lives all point to a spoiled individual who is not a capable person in any way. Nor are his relationships with people natural. He is a poor boss to his 300 servants and has the problem that people treat him differently simply because of who he is. He is also not a good judge of character as was clearly shown in his relationship with Laurens van der Post. He is also used to the good life and for all his speaking out on a range of issues he does not seem to be a man who has **the courage of his own convictions**. **To put it bluntly** his relationships with other people complicate his life even further as is best shown by the fact that he cannot marry the woman he loves yet does not have the ability to give up everything for her. He is weak and seemingly helpless. The only good thing the article has to say about Prince Charles is that none of this is his own fault.

Translation

Warum die Königin/Queen uns alle herunterzieht.
Über die Marotten der königlichen Familie zu schreiben, ist für mich etwas Neues. Vor zehn Tagen war ich im Begriff, aus der Kampagne für ein gewähltes Staatsoberhaupt zurückzutreten – wegen ihrer Einstellung gegenüber dem Privatleben der Windsors, wie sie sich offenbarte, als ‚Panorama*' die Aussichten von Camilla Parker Bowles, Königin zu werden, untersuchte. Die simulierte Ausschusssitzung der Unterstützungsgruppe zeigte eine unerträglich zynische Herangehensweise an die Sache, eine Republik ins Leben zu rufen. Der Vorsitzende, Professor Stephen Haseler, gab kund, dass in den Bemühungen, die Erbmonarchie zu beenden, das Benehmen des Prince of Wales ausgeschöpft werden müsse. Meine Argumente für ein gewähltes Staatsoberhaupt

waren schon immer auf die Unzulänglichkeit der Institution gegründet, nicht auf die Mängel des Einzelnen. Natürlich sah ich ein, dass das Erbprinzip auf der Idee von einer genetisch besonderen Familie basiert, wobei alles, was diese Familie tut – ob privat oder in der Öffentlichkeit – Beweise für ihre Eignung zur Herrschaft bietet. Aber ich war gegen die Monarchie, weil sie die Idee von einer sozialen Hierarchie verkörperte und die Nation aufforderte, zurückzublicken, anstatt nach vorne zu schauen – nicht, weil der Thronfolger kindische und unzüchtige Telefonanrufe tätigte.

** britische Fernsehsendung*

Composition

1. *As a supporter of constitutional monarchy in Britain you have been asked by the editor of the Times to write a short article outlining the reasons why Britain should retain a monarch as well as the reforms needed to stop the constitutional monarchy becoming a thing of the past.*

For this composition question it is important that
- you know a good deal about **constitutional monarchy**, how to define it, how it works, its history, and so on.
- you sound as if you believe in, or are opposed to the monarchy. You are either defending or attacking the King or Queen.
- you use **facts or historical or current examples** to support your claims.
- you keep in mind which newspaper you are writing for.

To any objective observer the monarchy is clearly good for Britain. We are all aware of the benefits tourism gets from the monarchy but people forget how envious many countries are of a land that has a Queen that is head of state, an official representative on important occasions and an advisor with a wide knowledge of foreign affairs. Yet some people would remove the monarchy in this country. In recent decades the calls to end constitutional monarchism in Britain have grown louder. If we are not careful the constitutional monarchy – a monarchy governed by a constitution that limits and defines the powers of a king or queen – will die a very quick death. If the constitutional monarchy is to survive this century it must become more active and be reformed. And therein lies the problem – how is that to be done? Currently the Queen's most important functions are probably the signing of bills, the holding of the Queen's speech and her consultations with the Prime Minister. How can the monarch become more active in political life? The answer lies in exercising her power more frequently and in a reform of the selection process of the monarch.

I would suggest that the monarch should take a more active role in the selection of the Lord Chancellor. Currently, she follows the Prime Minister's advice on this matter. This would increase both the independence of the monarch and of the judiciary from the political system. If a success she could then more directly influence the choice of other positions, that of bishops for example. The major reform needed however is in the way we select our monarch. The suitability of Prince Charles as the next king has been much debated. Likewise the unfairness of the hereditary system is a major argument used by republicans against monarchy. Why not allow an elected House of Lords choose the next monarch? This would preserve the legitimacy of the monarchy in the eyes of the people. One could either allow the House of Lords choose anybody at all they consider qualified or somebody from one family e. g. the current Royal Family. William – and not Charles – could be become king until death. These reforms would undoubtedly increase the popularity of the monarch. Whatever reforms are chosen, our monarch, the defender of liberty in Britain, must take a more active role in political life here. Much as we supporters of the monarchy may dislike it, the monarchs of the future must take a leaf out of the books of our populist 21st century politicians if the monarchy is to survive. Otherwise those self-same politicians may do away with Britain's most valued asset. And that is something nobody in their right minds would want for this fair land of ours.

2. *Choose one famous king, queen or member of a royal family whose life you consider to have been a good example of why there should not be a monarchical head of state in England. Write an essay on monarchy in which you highlight the failings of your chosen monarch and compare the position of the current queen to that of the German Bundestag President.*

If you decide to choose this question rather than the other composition question it is important that

- you know a good deal about **the life of the monarch** you choose.
- you are able to cite at least **three differences** between the queen's functions and those of the German President.

- you ask yourself what arguments supporters of the monarchy would make and counteract them in the course of your essay
- you structure your answer and **check your spelling and style** after you have finished.

In my opinion the reign of Henry VIII is the best example of why England would be better served with an elected head of state. Henry VIII succeeded to the throne in 1509 and reigned until 1547. He is most famous for the number of wives he had, many of whom he had executed or who died in childbirth in an attempt to give him the male heir to the throne he so desired. Although some have claimed he was a strong and ruthless ruler what they are really referring to is the fact that he had anybody killed who stood in his way. These included Thomas Cromwell and Thomas More. His reign caused strong Protestant Catholic divisions to emerge in Britain and a great deal of both his own wealth and the wealth of the monasteries was spent on wars during his time on the throne. He was all in all a distinctly dislikeable individual.

The serious arguments in favour of monarchy can be swiftly outlined and dismissed. It is said that the monarchy attracts money from tourism, provides a theoretical check to the power of the Commons and that the monarch is a non-political ambassador for Britain. The monarchy of course takes far more money from the people in taxes than it brings in by way of tourist revenue and does very little to check the power of Commons. It is non-political but when one considers the various stupid mistakes and blunders that people such as Prince Philip, Prince Charles and other members of the Royal family have made then one has to say they are not good ambassadors and it is time to get rid of the monarchy.

It is interesting to compare the monarch's role with that of an office such as President of Germany. The monarch is there for his or her life, for good – or for bad – as in Henry's case. The German president is only in office for a certain period of time. The monarch becomes king or queen by birthright, the German President is elected to his position, a much fairer way of producing a head of state and one more likely to ensure a well-qualified person gets the job. It is interesting to note in this context that all three of the most recent German presidents have been considered a success. The German President has less power than the Queen which is a good thing and his function is primarily a representative one. All these factors are good reasons why Britain should get rid of the monarch and elect a head of state instead.

Watson: 'Honest Jim' tells Roger Highfield about his hopes for human genetic enhancement

James Watson is one of the most passionate advocates of DNA manipulation, not just of plants and animals but of people, too. Even though no one knows the final destination of the DNA revolution, he wants us all to get there double quick. The youngest of the double helix Nobel laureates, Watson remains the most influential and will be feted in April at an anniversary dinner in London, at which the Prime Minister and other luminaries have been invited to toast the 1953 breakthrough. Watson's artless candour long ago earned him the nickname "Honest Jim". He made headlines for inviting Posh and Becks to the dinner, and for suggesting that plump black people have better sex lives than the model Kate Moss. Of his work as a fundraiser, he said: "I really like rich people"; and, describing his colleague, remarked: "I have never seen Francis Crick in a modest mood."

As a schoolboy growing up in Chicago, Watson was small, unathletic, and shy. He was also unpopular, and often bullied. His consolation lay in books and he was one of the junior geniuses who wrestled with brain twisters on The Quiz Kids, a halfhour radio show. In 1940, at the age of 12, he was confirmed. But, disillusioned by the war and how religious explanations seemed to be "myths from the past", he gave up mass to go birdwatching: "I came to the conclusion that the Church was just a bunch of fascists that supported Franco. I stopped going on Sunday mornings and watched the birds with my father instead."

His interest in ornithology would evolve, through a fascination with the then mystery of migration, into science. Like the other DNA pioneers, he was also deeply influenced as a teenager by Erwin Schrödinger's book *What is Life?,* which suggested the idea of a molecular code that carried genetic information. Even though Watson entered the University of Chicago precociously, as a 15 year old, his search for a graduate school almost came to nothing. Caltech turned him down. Harvard accepted him, though with no financial help. But he did make it to Indiana, which was strong in genetics.

He moved to Sir Lawrence Bragg's biophysics unit of the Cavendish Laboratory in Cambridge in 1951. After the triumphant discovery with Crick, Watson did not rest on his DNA laurels. He decided to leave Cambridge, despite its overwhelming influence on biology at that time. "Francis being such a dominant person, I had to. My own career demanded I separate from Francis." He would become an intellectual impresario, turning Cold Spring Harbor Laboratory on the East Coast of America, where he is now president, into one of the world's principal centres of biology and leading the effort to read the human genetic code.

Today, Watson believes in designer babies because he has faith in human genes in particular, those that underpin our ability to care for one another. He argues that much of the public paranoia surrounding human genetic manipulation is inspired by a legitimate recognition of our selfish side, where one person benefits at the expense of others. But this is only half the story: humans do not only compete, they cooperate and care for each other. In his new book, DNA: The Secret of Life, he goes further: "So fundamental is it to human nature that I am sure that the capacity to love is inscribed in our DNA. A secular Paul would say that love is the greatest gift of our genes to humanity."

The constellation of genes that makes us love one another will protect us. "Love, that impulse which promotes our caring for one another, is what has permitted our survival and success on the planet. It is this impulse that I believe will safeguard our future as we venture into uncharted genetic territory." By uncharted territory, he means the use of genetic manipulation to alter plants, animals and even people. "If, some day, the genes linked with love could be enhanced by our science, to defeat petty hatreds and violence, in what sense would our humanity be diminished?"

Watson is dismayed by the angst over GM technology, spurred by pressure groups "who raise money by raising fears". But even many of his peers are convinced that scientists should never attempt germline gene therapy, where the consequences of GM are passed to future generations. "Whether based in ethics or unfounded fears of the unknown, such arguments are ultimately not compelling, in my judgment. Germ line therapy is, in principle, simply putting right what chance has put horribly wrong."

Germ line gene therapy has the potential for making humans resistant to the ravages of HIV. Some say we should focus on education about the dangers of promiscuous sex. "I find such a moralistic response to be profoundly immoral," Watson says. "Education has proven a powerful but hopelessly insufficient weapon in our war."

Indeed, Watson goes further, advocating genetic enhancement. "Having identified the relevant genes, would we want to exercise a future power to transform slow learners into fast ones, before they are even born? We are not dealing in science fiction: we can already give mice better memories. Is there a reason why our goal shouldn't be to do the same for humans?

"All parents want to enhance their kids. I think you can be against it only because we can do it." Is that influenced in any way by anguish over his own son, Rufus, who has a mental disorder?

"I am very much wanting people to have healthy children." And he is passionate that this kind of decision should be down to the individual, not the state. Despite being pro germ line therapy, he is not in favour of cloning. "You want a law. You don't want 50 people looking like Gwyneth Paltrow." 965 words

© Telegraph Group Limited, 2003

Annotations

Posh and Becks (line 8): Victoria and David Beckham
Erwin Schrödinger (line 24): Austrian physicist (1887–1961) and discoverer of the wave equation.
Caltech (line 28): The California Institute of Technology
Germline gene therapy (line 58): This is a novel scientific approach that delivers genes to sperm or egg or to the cells that produce them. Gene therapy treats disease by "repairing" dysfunctional genes or by providing copies of missing genes and may yet cure or prevent disease by changing the expression of a person's genes.
Gwyneth Paltrow (line 79): Welsh actress

Worksheet: *Watson:* 'Honest Jim' tells Roger Highfield about his hopes for human genetic enhancement

Comprehension

1. What do you think were the factors that made James Watson unpopular at school?
2. Outline the role of religion in James Watson's childhood and its importance for his later career?
3. What do we learn from the text about Watson's relationship with his scientific colleagues and peers?

Analysis

Choose *one* of the following tasks. Write 200–300 words.

1. Summarise the arguments for and against human genetic manipulation as outlined in the text. Be careful to use your own words as far as possible.
2. Characterise the personality James Watson as he is known today from what we read about him in the text and the language he uses.

Composition

Choose *one* of the following tasks. Write a minimum of 200–300 words.

1. Script: A discovery that changed the world.
   As a writer for a TV programme on the History Channel it is your job to write a 300 word script commemorating a famous day of discovery, of scientific advancement or of technological change. Your script should consist of a title, a text, as well as anything else you think important e. g. video or audio input instructions.
2. Article: Genetically-modified crops
   In protest at the growth of genetically-modified crops a young woman throws rotten eggs at a number of the ministers entering Downing Street before a meeting of the Cabinet. After interviewing the protestor your task is to write up an article describing the incident and the arguments for and against genetically-modified food in Britain.

Key: Watson: 'Honest Jim' tells Roger Highfield about his hopes for human genetic enhancement

Comprehension

1. *What do you think were the factors that made James Watson unpopular at school?*

   A number of factors made James Watson unpopular at school. First of all, his physical appearance was not an asset to him. He was small and unathletic which **made him an obvious target for bullies. As a result** he was picked on by bigger and older students. In addition to this **he was a shy person who had the misfortune to be** very bright as a student. He was so good at school that he was able for the quiz questions on the radio. This would have turned the spotlight on him and made a lot of other students jealous of him. Although the text maintains he was a shy boy it is also quite possible that Watson's comments got him into trouble then as they have done in the course of his career since. **All these factors account for** his unpopularity while at school.

2. *Outline the role of religion in James Watson's childhood and its importance for his later career?*

   One should not make the mistake of underestimating the role religion played in his childhood and later career. He was confirmed at the age of 12 and in his early childhood used go to church every Sunday morning. As he grew older this strong influence changed. He came more under the influence of his father, who was interested in ornithology, and also began to have difficulty accepting the outdated and old-fashioned explanations offered by the church for many of the questions that most troubled him. He was also aware of the important role played by the church in the Spanish Civil War and he wrote the church off as nothing more than a "bunch of fascists". It sounds as if he was influenced by his father in this respect also though the text does not confirm or deny this. **What we can safely take for granted is** the fact that as he grew more and more interested in science and nature so his trust in religion waned. Eventually he turned his back on the church. The role of religion in his later career is a curious one. Religion was important for his later career more by its absence than by its presence. The fact that he had turned to science and away from the church meant he was heading down a road that would keep him firmly on the side of science and would eventually bring him fame. In many ways his turning to science was his attempt to find answers to religious questions that the church could not provide him.

3. *What do we learn from the text about Watson's relationship with his scientific colleagues and peers?*

   The text informs us of his relationships with his colleagues in such a way as to make clear to the reader that these relationships were not always harmonious. In the case of Crick, it is obvious that they were unable to continue working together. He describes Crick as a dominant person, a person he had to leave. This suggests a clash of some sort and he makes one snide comment when he says "Have you ever seen Francis Crick in a modest mood?" It is quite clear that the two men did not get on. He also disagrees with some of his peers about GM technology. He disagrees with those who are wary of GM and considers their arguments unconvincing. From this and from the way he speaks he sounds like a very domineering character and a man who could be difficult to get on with.

Analysis

1. *Analyse the arguments for and against human genetic manipulation as outlined in the text. Be careful to use your own words as far as possible*

When asked to analyse the arguments in a text it is important to remember
- to examine the entire text in detail and look for all the relevant information.
- to come up with at least three points for and three against GM.
- to use your own words and not quote directly.

The text addresses this question indirectly but there are a number of arguments to be gleaned from it.
First of all genetic manipulation gives man the chance to repair or alter things that have gone wrong such as deformity, mental disorders or an illness like HIV. It also gives us the opportunity of turning slow learners into fast ones. Watson thinks this gives man the opportunity to correct what chance has brought about. This is something he is very much in favour of. Secondly, it gives parents the chance to have healthy children. Thirdly, it offers the prospect of removing hatred and violence from society. It allows humans the chance of caring more for one another. On the other hand, the text points out that many people, scientists amongst them, are simply being selfish and stupid when they reject GM. The text also says that in many cases this opposition to human genetic manipulation is just a way for people to earn money. The final argument the text makes against GM is that many people believe you should not pass on the results of such experimentation to future generations. In my opinion none of these arguments are convincing, a fact which reflects Watson's own convictions. It is possible that if an opponent of GM put them forward they would be more convincing but not as they stand here.

2. *Characterise the personality James Watson as he is known today from what we read about him in the text and the language he uses.*

When attempting this question
- ask yourself what kind of a person Jim Watson is.
- ask yourself why he is called Honest Jim.
- look carefully at the quotes in the text.
- think of a number of adjectives you would use to describe such a person.
- support your description with facts from the text.

As a person James Watson is a colourful, controversial, influential and well-known individual. He is influential and important in the sense that he is the president of a major centre for biology and research into the human genetic code. He is particularly well-known for repeatedly being in the headlines. The text cites a number of examples of this such as his decision to invite Posh and Becks to dinner and his belief in designer babies. His reference to the fact that fat black people have better sex lives than slim white models also made front-page news. His personality reveals a man who believes firmly in the opinions he holds, a man who sometimes goes over the top to make his point. In this text the language he uses always serves the purpose of driving home the beliefs he holds dearest e. g. when he wants to hit out at those opponents of germ line technology he says "I find such a moralistic response to be profoundly immoral" or "I think you can be against it only because we can do it." His clever use of words reveals an intelligent and witty person, as one might expect of such a famous scientist. Above all else he is his own man, straight out in all he says and does. This explains a comment such as "I really like rich people," coming as it does from a fundraiser. Even in this article he comes across as lively and full of ideas and both the language he uses and the career he has had reflect this.

Composition

1. *Script: A Discovery that changed the World*
   As a writer for a TV programme on the History Channel it is your job to write a 300 word script commemorating a famous day of discovery, of scientific advancement or of technological change. Your script should consist of a title, a text, as well as anything else you think important e.g. video or audio input instructions.

You should only attempt this question if you know a great deal about some particular discovery. Otherwise your account will be too skimpy. Also do not forget the following when answering this question:

- To come up with **a title** for the piece.
- To indicate **the length of time** it should take.
- To use a good number **of visual shots** to back up the text.
- To keep your description clear, to the point and **historically correct**.
- To show what influence the discovery has had on mankind and society in general.

History Channel:
Programme Title: It Happened This Week
Time: 2–3 minutes
Introduction: Shots of the horrors of World War II

Shot 1: Nazi Germany, Hitler, Bombing of London, Suffering Civilians
Text: (Voice 1) In the summer of 1940 it seemed as if Adolf Hitler would go on to conquer the whole of Europe. Countries such as Poland and France were already in his grasp. Could anything stop his path to power and total control of the European continent?
(Voice 2) The answer, as we now know, was yes and behind this answer is the forgotten story of the colourful group of brilliant scientists who created the microwave radar systems that not only helped win World War II but set off an explosion of scientific achievements and technological advances that have changed our daily lives.

Shot 2: Shot of an ocean liner in Liverpool, August 1940.
(Voice 2) At the height of the Battle of Britain, British scientists secretly accompanied a mysterious black box aboard a Canadian liner bound for the US. Inside was one of Britain's most closely guarded military secrets: a cavity magnetron, a radar transmitter that made the exact identification of military targets possible – even at night and during bad weather. The magnetron's arrival set off the most dramatic mobilization of science in history as America's top scientists joined the "war within the war" to change the British invention into a potent military weapon.

Shot 3: Actors acting out the arrival in Washington of a team of British scientists in September 1940. Shot of White House. Final shot of scientists working in the RadLab e. g. Jerome Wiesner.
(Voice 2) Leaving behind American pre-war isolationism, American and British scientists, working under the wings of American government and industry, founded the Radiation Lab at the Massachusetts Institute of Technology for exploring scientific applications for Britain's microwave research. Developed in top-secret and in a rush at the laboratory, microwave radars eventually helped destroy Japanese warships in the Pacific, brought down Nazi buzz bombs over England, and enabled Allied bombers to "see" through cloud cover over Germany and Japan.

Shot 4: Cheering crowds, D-Day, Peace.
(Voice 2) Although it was the atomic bomb that ended World War II, in many ways it was radar that won it. The Rad Lab was an incubator for science and technology on a scale perhaps unknown in history. The work of the microwave radar pioneers resulted in a whole range of technical advances in engineering that transformed our lives, ushering in as it did the presence of transistors, microwave ovens, and computers.

Closing Shot: People using modern gadgets or machines such as a microwave or computer.

2. *Article: Genetically-modified crops*
In protest at the growth of genetically-modified crops, a young woman throws rotten eggs at a number of ministers entering Downing Street before a meeting of the Cabinet. After interviewing the protestor your task is to write up an article describing the incident and the arguments for and against genetically-modified food in Britain.

When answering this question you should

- draw up a list of points **for and against** the topic in question.
- encorporate these points into your interview.
- decide on **the setting** for your interview.
- use **a number of quotes** from the interview to make it seem real.
- have the article come to **a definite conclusion** on the matter.

There was something ironic about the fact that the object which struck Environment Minister Ted Hall was a rotten egg. After all, this is a dispute about food and the after smell was unpleasant to say the least. The police grabbed hold of Helen Shaw quickly but those of us reporters who witnessed the scene were struck by the smile on her young face as a burly police constable pinned her to the ground. She is a woman of considerable determination as I found out to my good fortune two hours later when the police released her on bail. "An interview? Of course I'll give ye an interview, but only to the Guardian," she announced, to the considerable disgust of my colleagues from the Mirror and the Sun.
Sitting in a nearby pub, clearly excited by the fact that her picture would be all over the papers the next day, she made clear her opposition to GM food. "The most serious potential harm from growing genetically modified crops

in Britain is the effect on farmland wildlife not on humans", she sighed regretfully. "Repeated studies, including this latest review the government is choosing to ignore, show that there is a strong risk of potential cross-contamination. GM crops also damage fauna and flora far more than normal crops. "What makes you so committed to your cause?", I asked, after a pause in the conversation. "Some day I want to have children." she said. "I want a safe future for them." Hmm. "But what about the advantages of GM crops?" I ask. "Such as?" "Well," I stumbled, trying to recall what I knew from my research. "The reduction or elimination of hunger and poverty" "Yes," she replied, "but at what price." "Can you guarantee the safety of future generations?" "The risks to human health are very low", I continued. "The rewards are surely worth investigating. Think of Africa, the starving millions."
Suddenly she flared up, anger simmering in her eyes. "And think of all the weed killers that will be used on these crops. These are powerful herbicides that can do untold damage to children in the womb, not to mention their mothers and fathers. But you journalists are all the same. You want a story, an interview. You are not really interested in the facts, in highlighting the danger involved in GM food." And then she was gone. As explosively as she had entered my day, flinging a rotten egg at a Minister of the Crown. I tried to understand Helen Shaw's anger. I came to the conclusion she was either a crank or a committed environmental soldier, way before her time. Only the future generations will know the answer. And by that time GM crops will be as much part of our daily food as the sliced pan.

Glossary of literary terms

1. An **allegory** is a poem, play or story in which the characters and events are used to symbolize a **deeper moral or spiritual meaning.**

   Example: Typical allegories would be Bunyan's *Pilgrim's Progress* or George Orwell's *Animal Farm.* In *Animal Farm* the pigs represent a totalitarian regime.

2. **Alliteration:** Sometimes referred to as **head rhyme** or **initial rhyme**, alliteration is a term we use to describe the repetition of the initial sounds, usually consonants, in a line or poetry or in closely adjacent lines. Alexander Pope said "The sound must be an echo to the sense." by which he meant that a good poet uses alliteration not just because it sounds nice but because it reinforces the meaning and purpose of the lines in question. Alliteration therefore is used **to create melody, establish mood, or call attention to important words.** It also highlights similarities or contrasts.

   Example "Scooping spilt, soft, broken oil with a silver spoon from a flagstone floor. …"

   (M-M-Memory from The Other Country *by Carol Ann Duffy)*

3. **Allusion:** When a writer alludes to something in the course of writing a poem, he refers to information assumed to be known by the reader. This can be a reference to a person or a well-known occurrence such as a battle or war, a TV character or a well-known literary character.

   Example: "An old woman who looked like one of the witches from Macbeth" he said. This allusion was lost on Sally. Seeing her puzzlement he went on, "wrinkled, don't you know, and hideous and so forth" …

   (From: The Ruby in the Smoke *by Philip Pullman)*

4. **Ambiguity** is the state of being doubtful, unclear or indistinct. It is a characteristic of writing which makes something capable of being understood in more than one way. A poet will often do this deliberately.

   Example: A simple example of ambiguity is to be found in the sentence "They found me a good worker." This is ambiguous in that it has two meanings i.e. They found me to be a good worker or They found a good worker for me. The context is necessary for it to be properly understood. A writer making effective use of ambiguity will use language and context to leave something unclear or open to more than one interpretation.

5. **Analogy:** This term refers to **an agreement or similarity** in some things which are otherwise quite different from one another.

   Example: Sleep and death are not really similar but would be analogous in that both normally involve no movement and often happen when a person is in a lying position.

6. **Anaphora:** The repetition of a word or phrase at the start of a succession of phrases in order to achieve **rhetorical effect.** This is most commonly used in plays or famous speeches.

   Example: "*We shall fight* in France, *we shall fight* on the seas and oceans, *we shall fight* with growing confidence and growing strength in the air, *we shall* defend our island, whatever the cost may be, *we shall fight* on the beaches, *we shall fight* on the landing grounds, *we shall fight* in the fields and in the streets, *we shall fight* in the hills. *We shall* never surrender."
   (Winston Churchill)

7. **Antithesis:** refers to the exact opposite of something being highlighted in parallel words or in the juxtaposition of contrasting ideas or phrases.

   Example: Brutus: Not that I loved Caesar less, but that I loved Rome more.
   (Julius Caesar by William Shakespeare)

8. An **antonym** is a word which is the opposite of something else.

   Example: good – bad / easy – difficult.

9. An **aside** is a statement uttered in the course of a play which is intended for the ears of the audience only and is not heard by the other characters on stage at the time.

   Example: Macbeth "Thanks for that.
   (Aside) There the grown serpent lies, the worm that's fled. ..."
   (Macbeth by William Shakespeare)

10. **Assonance** refers to the use of the **same vowel sound with different consonants** or the same consonants with different vowels in successive words or stressed syllables.

    Example: time and light *or* mystery and mastery

11. **Blank Verse** is a term referring to verse which does not rhyme but which is written in a set metrical pattern e. g. **iambic pentameters** (i. e. an unstressed syllable followed by a stressed syllable in each poetic foot) Shakespeare used it frequently as did Milton in Paradise Lost and Wordsworth also used blank verse in his poetry. Blank verse is used extensively in **dramatic or narrative verse.**

    Example: "The qua / lity / of mer / cy is / not strain'd /
    It drop / peth as / the gen / tle rain / from heaven / "
    (The Merchant of Venice William Shakespeare)

12. **Characterisation** refers to the method an author uses to present his characters to the reader. This may involve **physical description,** an account of **speech and behaviour,** a character's **opinions and reactions,** or finally, what a character **feels or thinks** about something.

    Example: Frances Lennox was a minor, steady, reliable actress, and had never been asked for anything more. This part was in a brilliant new play, a two-hander, and the male part would be taken by Tony Wilde who until now had seemed so far above her she would never have had the ambition to think of her name and his side by side on a poster ...
    (The Sweetest Dream by Doris Lessing)

13. **Cliché** refers to words or phrases that have been used so often that they are more or less meaningless.

    Example As dead as a doornail. As cool as a cucumber.

14. **Climax:** A group of sentences or clauses which starts with the weakest and then builds to a high point in order to achieve effect. The term can also refer to the high point of a story or play.

    Example: "It is an outrage to bind a Roman citizen; to scourge him is an atrocious crime; to put him to death is almost a parricide; but to crucify him, what shall I call it?"
    (Cicero)

15. The term **conflict** is used when talking about a problem or struggle between two opposing forces in a story. The main types of conflicts which occur are: person against person, person against self, person against society and person against nature.

    Example: One of the central themes of *How to be Good* by Nick Hornby is the struggle the main character experiences between the person she is and the person she wants to be. This conflict is the main driving force behind her story.

16. **Consonance:** The repeating of specific consonant sounds after different vowel sounds.

    Example: Consonance is the similarity between consonants, but not between vowels, as between the s and t sounds in "sweet silent thought"

17. **Elements of fiction:** This term refers to certain aspects of a literary work. A criticism or analysis of a book or story might concentrate on any of the following elements: **the action, the antagonist** (i. e. the person or force that works against the **protagonist** or hero of the story), the **characters**, the **climax**, the **conflict**, the **dialogue**, the **exposition,** (i. e. the part of the story in which the characters first appear, the background is explained and the setting is described), the **falling action** (i. e. the action and dialogue following the climax that lead the reader into the story's end), the **mood**, the **moral**, the **narrator**, the **plot**, the **resolution**, (i. e. how everything turns out), the **rising action** (i. e. the central part of the story during which various problems arise after a conflict is introduced), the **setting**, the **style** and the **theme**.

    Example: The theme of the short story collection, *Dubliners,* by James Joyce is essentially one of life and human nature in Dublin as seen through the eyes of the characters involved.

18. Ellipsis is a stylistic device used to achieve poetic effect whereby the poet omits a word or phrase which is easily known to the reader.

Example: In the following example the word 'go' has been omitted between 'shall' and 'along' – "And he to England shall along with you."
(Hamlet by William Shakespeare 3.3.1)

19. An **epigram** is **a witty paradoxical remark.** Oscar Wilde was famous for his epigrams.

Example: "A poet can survive everything but a misprint." or "I can resist everything but temptation."
(Oscar Wilde)

20. A **euphemism** is a polite phrase or word which is used to say something that is considered unpleasant or hurtful in a nice and acceptable manner.

Example: China is a country where you often get different accounts of the same thing *(where many lies are told)* or He passed away = *(he died ...)*

21. Figurative language takes in such devices as **simile, hyperbole, personification** and **metaphor.**

Example: "He clasps the crag with crooked hands
Close to the sun in lonely lands
Ringed with the azure world, he stands."
(The Eagle by Lord Tennyson)

22. Foreshadowing happens when the author gives hints about things which will later come to pass in the course of a story.

Example: In *Julius Caesar* by William Shakespeare, Caesar's wife has nightmares in which she foresees his death.
Act II Scene II
Thunder and lightning. Enter CAESAR, in his night-gown
"Nor heaven nor earth have been at peace to-night:
Thrice hath Calphurnia in her sleep cried out,
'Help, ho! they murder Caesar!' Who's within?" ...

23. **Flashback** is the opposite of foreshadowing. It is an interruption in the action of a story or work of non-fiction to show an episode that happened at an earlier time. A flashback is usually used to provide background information necessary to an understanding of the characters of a plot.

Example: In *The Snows of Kilimanjaro*, Harry Street, who is dying, becomes preoccupied with incidents in his past. In a flashback Street remembers one of his wartime comrades dying painfully on barbed wire on a battlefield in Spain.

24. **Hyperbole** is an **exaggerated form** of language which is used to increase effect.

Example: I could eat a horse or All the perfume of Arabia could not sweeten this little hand

(Macbeth by William Shakespeare)

25. **Imagery:** When we speak about imagery we are referring to those elements in a poem which evoke mental pictures not just visual ones but emotional ones also. Many images are conveyed by figurative language such as **similes, metaphors and personification.**

Example: When the evening is spread out against the sky
Like a patient etherized upon a table.

(The Love Song of J. Alfred Prufrock - T. S. Eliot)

26. **Irony** involves the humorous use of words to imply the opposite of what they actually mean. Irony is a question of the contrast between what seems to be and what actually is. We speak of **verbal irony, dramatic irony, irony of situation** and **irony of tone.**

Example: Moments after Eileen shot herself, having earlier been told that John, her husband, had been killed in the war, he came walking up the drive with his rucksack over his shoulder.

27. When we speak of **literary forms** we are talking about various types of writing. These include such well-known types as comedy, drama, essay, historical fiction novel, poetry, science fiction and the short story. Other

literary forms include myth, folktale, autobiography, biography, realistic fiction and prose.

Example: The novel *The Time Machine* by H.G. Wells is a good example of early science fiction writing.

28. **Mood:** The overall emotional effect created by a poem or other piece of literature.

    Example: The mood created in the poem Originally (Carol Ann Duffy) is a reflective one, one full of memories and uncertainty. The poet is considering a time when she lived in a different country and is wondering where she actually comes from. The conclusion of the poem reads "And I hesitate", a finish which contributes to, and is typical of, the overall mood of the poem.

29. The word **paradox** refers to a seemingly absurd or self-contradictory statement that is or may be true.

    Example: What a pity that youth must be wasted on the young.
    (George Bernard Shaw)

30. **Personification** is the attribution of human qualities to something which is not human.

    Example: An example of this might be "As the wind undressed the trees, fear grabbed at his throat..."
    or "The plane began to creak and protest as it fought its way through the storm."

31. **Plot** is the pattern of action in a short story, novel or play. Plot usually deals with a conflict and this conflict may be internal or external. In a book with a good plot all the details are important and are arranged so that the outcome depends on each one and the interaction of all the details with one another. The plot may have **a protagonist** who is opposed by an **antagonist**, creating what is known as **conflict**. A plot may include flashback or it may include a subplot which is a mirror image of the main plot.

Example: In Shakespeare's, *King Lear,* the relationship between the Earl of Gloucester and his sons mirrors the relationship between Lear and his daughters

32. **Point of View** refers to the writer's choice of narrator for his story. A writer has three basic choices when it comes to deciding on what point of view will be used in a novel.

Example: Personal or first-person: the narrator "I" is a character in the story who can reveal only his own thoughts and what he sees and is told. *Robinson Crusoe* is told from a first-person point of view. Third person objective is where the narrator is an outsider who can report only what he sees and hears. An example would be *Hard Times* by Charles Dickens.
An omniscient point of view is where the narrator knows everything and can enter the minds of his characters. He may enter the minds of all the characters or the mind of just one if he wishes to focus on one character. Joyce's *Ulysses* is told in this manner.

33. A **pun** is **a play on words** in which words are used to exploit ambiguities in meaning, usually for humorous effect.

Example: Ben Battle was a soldier bold and used to war's alarms
But a cannonball took off his legs so he laid down his arms.

34. **Repetition** is one of the most frequently used stylistic devices and simply involves the frequent use of the same word or phrase in a piece of writing.

Example: "You cannot sir, take from me anything that I would more willingly part withal, except my life, except my life, except my life."
(Hamlet by William Shakespeare)

35. **Rhetoric** refers to the effective use of language, particularly in a **speech**, when one is trying to persuade someone or convert them to one's opinion.

Example: "Friends, Romans, countrymen
Lend me your ears
I come…"
(Julius Caesar by William Shakespeare)

36. A **rhetorical question** is one to which no answer is required because the answer is clear from the question which has been posed.

Example: Who knows? (The answer nobody knows is clear from the question itself)

37. **Rhyme** is a term we use to describe the repetition of syllable sounds. We speak of **end rhyme** and **internal rhyme.** The pattern created by rhyme in a poem is referred to the rhyming scheme.

Example: "I'm a lean dog, a keen dog, a wild dog and lone;
I'm a rough dog, a tough dog, hunting on my own"
(Irene Rutherford McLeod)

38. **Sarcasm** is a particular type of irony. Sarcasm is usually intended to be aggressive and is often insulting and aimed at a person. Sarcasm, it is sometimes said, is the lowest form of wit.

Example: "You are a wonderful goalkeeper." (To someone who has just conceded 9 goals in a match …)

39. **Satire:** A literary work which exposes and ridicules human folly and uses **sarcasm, wit** and **irony** to do so. It is usually directed against the injustice of social wrongs e. g. poverty, corruption.

Example: Famous satirists would include Dryden, Swift, Pope and Orwell. *Animal Farm* (Orwell) and *Gulliver's Travels* (Swift) are among the most famous works of satire ever written.

40. **Setting** is the time and place in which the events of a story or novel take place.

Example: The book *Ulysses*, by Irish writer James Joyce, has perhaps the most well-known setting of any modern novel. It is set in Dublin on one particular day in 1904, a day that has since become known as Bloomsday in honour of a character, Leopold Bloom, who appears in the book. The setting in Act 1, Scene 1 of Shakespeare's *Romeo and Juliet* is a public square in Verona, Italy.

41. **Simile** is a comparison of two completely different objects using "**like**" or "**as**". It is not generally considered as powerful as a metaphor since it does not defy logic.

Example: "Errors, like straws, upon the surface flow …" (Nesfield)

42. **Soliloquy:** This is **a speech** which is spoken by a character in a play at a time when he or she is unaccompanied on the stage.

Example: The best-known soliloquy in the English language is Hamlet's speech in which he utters his famous "to be or not to be …" statement.

43. The **sonnet** has its origins in the time of Petrarch and Michelangelo. It moved to France in the sixteenth century and arrived in England via the work of Wyatt and Surrey. It is a fixed poetic form of fourteen lines in iambic pentameter. In the Elizabethan or Shakespearean sonnet the lines are divided into three quatrains and a couplet (abab, cdcd, efef, gg) The original Italian form is divided into an octave of two rhyme-sounds following an abba abba pattern and a sestet of two additional rhyme patterns cdc, dcd or cde,cde. Eventually, the ability to write a sonnet became part of a wealthy man's education.

Example: Shakespeare's *Shall I compare thee to a summer's day?* is one of the most famous sonnets.

44. **Stream of consciousness**: A **narrative technique** developed towards the end of the 19th century used to portray and evoke the psychic life of a character and depict subjective as well as objective reality. Stream of consciousness refers to the presentation of a character's thoughts, feelings, actions and so on.

Example: In his work *The Butcher Boy* the Irish author Patrick McCabe uses the first person stream of consciousness to show his main character's descent into madness.

45. **Symbol:** This is a word which stands for or is somehow connected to an idea and is therefore a sign of something.

Example: Union Jack – Britain. In Robert Frost's poem *Acquainted with the Night* both the night and darkness are symbols for death or depression.

46. **Tautology** refers to the repetition of an idea in different words, phrases or in a sentence.

Example: With malice toward none, with charity for all.
(Second Inaugural Address – A. Lincoln)

47. **Theme** refers to a unifying motif in, or the main meaning of, a work and this is often a general truth about life. A theme can be stated directly or implied.

Example: One of the main themes of Edna O'Brien's collection of short stories *Lantern Slides* is the confinement provincial life in Ireland places upon those who live there.

48. **Tone:** When a reader refers to the tone of a poem he or she is usually speaking about **the writer's attitude** to the subject he is writing about. More specifically it can refer to **the moral outlook** of a piece. Tone is sometimes used to describe the overall feeling of a poem and thus is closely related to the mood.

Example: The tone of the book *Cannery Row* by John Steinbeck is objective, neutral and non-judgemental. The writer does not express disapproval of the actions of Mack and his band.

49. The word **tragedy** is primarily used at a literary level to refer to **a medieval narrative poem** or **a Renaissance drama** in which the downfall of a great person be it a king, an emperor or a good person is the main theme of the work.

Example: *Julius Caesar* and *King Lear* both describe the downfall of great individuals and are among the greatest tragedies ever written.

50. **Understatement:** is a comment made in a restrained and somehow less important way to achieve heightened effect and increase the actual importance of what is being said. This is often done in an ironic way.

Example: After Macbeth murders his friend Banquo, he goes on to play down the deed by referring to the number of people who have been murdered since the beginning of time, saying "Blood hath been shed ere now."

STARK Lernhilfen nach der neuen Prüfungsordnung!

Sicher durch das neue Abitur!

Abitur-Training Baden-Württemberg

Effektive Abitur-Vorbereitung zum selbstständigen Training: Klare Fakten, prägnante Beispiele, Übungsaufgaben auf Abiturniveau mit erklärenden Lösungen zur Selbstkontrolle.
Die Bände der Reihe Abitur-Training Baden-Württemberg sind auf die neuen Bildungspläne abgestimmt:

NEU Analysis I – (Pflichtteil) .... Best.-Nr. 84001
NEU Analysis II – (Wahlteil) .... Best.-Nr. 84002
NEU Analytische Geometrie .... Best.-Nr. 84003
NEU Englisch – Textaufgaben .... Best.-Nr. 84468
NEU Geschichte 1 .... Best.-Nr. 84761
NEU Geschichte 2 .... Best.-Nr. 84762
NEU Biologie 1 – Molekular- und Zellbiologie Genetik Neuro- und Immunbiologie .... Best.-Nr. 84701
NEU Biologie 2 – Stammesgeschichtliche Entwicklung des Lebens · Biotechnologie .... Best.-Nr. 84702
NEU Chemie 1 – Energetik · Gleichgewichte · Säuren und Basen · Elektrochemie .... Best.-Nr. 84731
NEU Chemie 2 – Biomoleküle · Aromatische Verbindungen · Kunststoffe .... Best.-Nr. 84732

Lexikon

Ideal für Schülerinnen und Schüler zum Nachschlagen im Unterricht, bei der Vorbereitung von Referaten, fundierten Diskussionen, Facharbeiten oder Projekten.

Lexikon Autoren und Werke .... Best.-Nr. 944081
Lexikon Biologie .... Best.-Nr. 94711
Lexikon Geschichte .... Best.-Nr. 94787
Lexikon Erdkunde .... Best.-Nr. 94904
Lexikon Politik/Sozialkunde .... Best.-Nr. 94801
Lexikon Ethik und Religion .... Best.-Nr. 94959

Interpretationshilfen zu Pflichtlektüren

Die optimale Vorbereitung auf das **Abitur 2004** in Baden-Württemberg: Interpretationshilfen zu den **aktuellen Pflichtlektüren** („Sternchenthemen“) für Deutsch ***Kabale und Liebe*** und ***Effi Briest*** sowie für Englisch ***Moon Palace***. Mit Informationen zu Autor und Werk, ausführlicher Inhaltsangabe und einer systematischen Interpretation des Textes.

Friedrich Schiller: *Kabale und Liebe* .... Best.-Nr. 2400231
Theodor Fontane: *Effi Briest* .... Best.-Nr. 2400371
Paul Auster: *Moon Palace* .... Best.-Nr. 2500031

(Bitte blättern Sie um)

STARK Lernhilfen nach der neuen Prüfungsordnung!

Sicher durch das neue Abitur!

Das neue Abitur 2004 Baden-Württemberg

Auch für die neuen Prüfungsanforderungen in Baden-Württemberg gibt es die bewährten Vorbereitungsbücher. Die neuen Bände enthalten:

- Hinweise zum neuen Abitur (Worauf kommt es an? Was ist neu?)
- Zusätzlich eine Auswahl von Abituraufgaben der letzten Jahre mit Themen, die für die Prüfung 2004 weiterhin relevant sind bzw. den neuen Anforderungen angepasst wurden
- Übungsaufgaben im neuen Abiturstil
- Alle Aufgaben mit Lösungen

NEU	Abiturprüfung BW Mathematik	Best.-Nr. 85001
NEU	Abiturprüfung BW Physik	Best.-Nr. 85321
NEU	Abiturprüfung BW Deutsch	Best.-Nr. 85401
NEU	Abiturprüfung BW Englisch	Best.-Nr. 85461
NEU	Abiturprüfung BW Französisch	Best.-Nr. 85501
NEU	Abiturprüfung BW Latein	Best.-Nr. 85601
NEU	Abiturprüfung BW Erdkunde	Best.-Nr. 85901
NEU	Abiturprüfung BW Geschichte	Best.-Nr. 85761
NEU	Abiturprüfung BW Gemeinschaftskunde	Best.-Nr. 85801
NEU	Abiturprüfung BW Biologie	Best.-Nr. 85701
NEU	Abiturprüfung BW Chemie	Best.-Nr. 85731
NEU	Abiturprüfung BW Ethik	Best.-Nr. 85951

Kompakt-Wissen

Prüfungsrelevantes Wissen in Kompaktform, als Gedächtnisstütze. An treffenden Beispielen verdeutlicht und grafisch veranschaulicht.

Kompakt-Wissen Abitur Analysis	Best.-Nr. 900151
Kompakt-Wissen Abitur Wahrscheinlichkeitsrechnung und Statistik	Best.-Nr. 900351
Kompakt-Wissen Abitur Analytische Geometrie	Best.-Nr. 900251
Kompakt-Wissen Algebra	Best.-Nr. 90016
Kompakt-Wissen Geometrie	Best.-Nr. 90026
Kompakt-Wissen Kurzgrammatik – Englisch	Best.-Nr. 90461
Kompakt-Wissen Wortschatz – Englisch	Best.-Nr. 90462
Kompakt-Wissen Abitur Politik/Sozialkunde	Best.-Nr. 948001

13-VIT

Bestellungen bitte direkt an:
STARK Verlagsgesellschaft mbH & Co. KG · Postfach 1852 · 85318 Freising
Telefon: 08161/179-0 · Telefax: 08161/179-51 · www.stark-verlag.de · info@stark-verlag.de

STARK